SEW YOUR OWN

BAGS & ACCESSORIES

SEW 19 STUNNING PROJECTS
EXPLAINED STEP BY STEP

SUPPORTED BY VIDEOS

SHUFUNO MISHIN

FULL SIZE
PATTERN
SHEET
INSERT

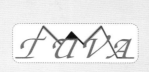

CONTENTS

CHAPTER **1** EASY ACCESSORIES

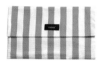  

1 ONE PIECE WALLETS
▶ Page 6

2 FLAT BUT THICK WALLET
▶ Page 12

3 BAG WITH ORIGINAL
AND CLEVER HANDLES
▶ Page 14

4 POUCHES WITH POCKET
▶ Page 16

5 SMART WALLET
▶ Page 18

CHAPTER **2** CLEVER BAGS AND WALLETS

6 TRAPEZOIDAL BOSTON MINI BAGS
▶ Page 20

7 MULTIPOCKET YOKE BAGS
▶ Page 22

8 **BELLOWS WALLET AND BAG**
▶ Page 24

9 **MULTIPOCKET FLAT BAG**
▶ Page 32

10 **TRAPEZOIDAL POUCHES**
▶ Page 34

11 **"SHELL" POUCHES**
▶ Page 35

12 **BAG WITH ROUNDED OPENING**
▶ Page 36

13 **MULTIPOCKET TOTES**
▶ Page 38

CHAPTER **3** CLEVER AND PRACTICAL ACCESSORIES

14 **VANITY CASE**
▶ Page 41

15 **STORAGE BOXES**
▶ Page 42

Three uses of metal reinforcements

16 **WALLET WITH A TAB**
▶ Page 44

17 **MINI BAG**
▶ Page 44

18 **WALL STORAGE BOXES**
▶ Page 45

19 **PENCIL CASES**
▶ Page 46

1 The instructions are available on the YouTube channel

The URL and the QR code are indicated at the bottom of the photos of the final products.

- An advertisement may be inserted before the video.
- Some written explanations are slightly different from those on video.

2 Commercial Use Possible

It is possible to sell products made from the patterns in this book

- The sale is authorized only for individuals but not for companies.
- It is forbidden to sell patterns, instructions or to make kits.
- It is forbidden to publish the instructions filmed and / or photographed on the internet.

3 DIFFICULTY

The difficulty of each project is indicated.

- The difficulty is an indicative measure.

★☆☆☆☆
Easy

★★★★★
Difficult

CHAPTER 1

EASY ACCESSORIES

Rectangular pieces, straight seams, flat patterns... The projects in this chapter are super easy to make. Despite their simplicity, they still contain a lot of interesting tips.

a

b

c

1 ONE PIECE WALLETS

Would you expect that these wallets with their clever pocket were made from a single piece of fabric? Cotton fabric is chosen for models a and c, and waterproof polyester for model b.

https://youtu.be/A3GkIw42Gwk

Instructions: P. 8

Prepare a Rectangle
of Fabric

Very
Practical!

The waterproof fabric is perfect for a toiletry bag.

The zipper is attached
between
two layers of fabric.

There are two compartments, the front pocket has a zipper.

CONSTRUCTION OF WALLET

NO 1 PAGE 6

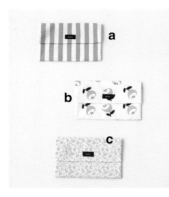

SUPPLIES (for 1 model, from left to right for models a / b / c)

22 x 92 cm striped cotton / polyester with flowers / cotton with lemon patterns (body of the wallet)
1 zipper - 20 cm long
1 label - 1.5 x 4.5 cm

Prepare only one piece of fabric

top stop

PREPARATION • A different thread is used here for better visibility.

1 SEW THE ZIPPER

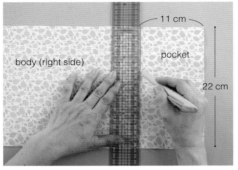

body (right side) — pocket — 11 cm — 22 cm

① Draw one line 11 cm from the right edge using a marker.②

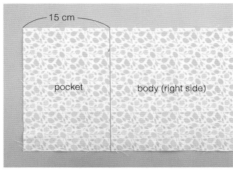

15 cm — pocket — body (right side)

② Draw one line 15 cm from the left edge using a marker.

zipper (wrong side) — pocket (right side) — 11 cm

① Place the zipper on the pocket mark, right sides together.

0.7 cm — pocket (wrong side) — Fold

② Fold the fabric over the pocket mark, then hold the assembly with clips. Draw one line 0.7 cm from the fold.

KEY POINT

Zipper Foot

One side of the foot is open so that the foot does not overlap the notches of the zipper.

③ Place the zipper foot, then sew.

④ In the middle of the seam, put the needle into the fabric, then raise the foot. Move the zipper so it is the foot.

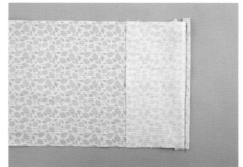

⑤ Continue to sew. The zipper is sewn.

⑥ Turn the fabric onto the right side, then iron.

⑦ Topstitch 0.2 cm from the edge.

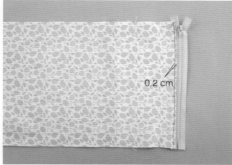

⑧ The topstitching is finished.

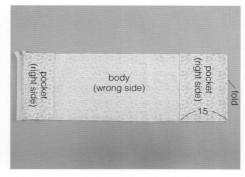

⑨ Turn the body on the wrong side. Fold the other pocket 15 cm from the edge, on the mark.

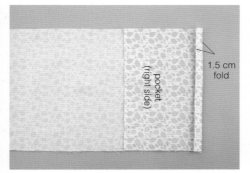

⑩ Fold again 1.5 cm.

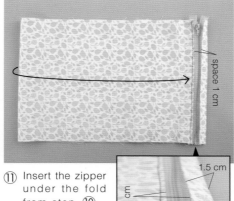
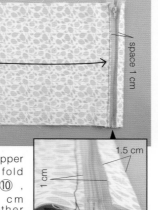

⑪ Insert the zipper under the fold from step ⑩, leaving 1 cm from the other edge.

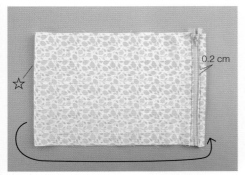

⑫ Hold the assembly with clips.

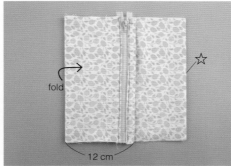

⑬ Sew 0.2 cm from the zipper. Fold the body with the edge indicated by ☆ to the right of the zipper.

2 ASSEMBLE THE SIDES

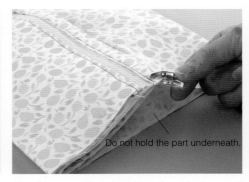

① Mark the fold 12 cm from the pocket.

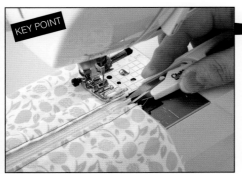

② Move aside one piece from below and place clips at the end of the zipper.

KEY POINT

The end of the zipper is pulled apart. Close the gap with pliers, and stitch in the machine.

③ Stitch 0.7 cm from the edge for 7 cm to assemble.

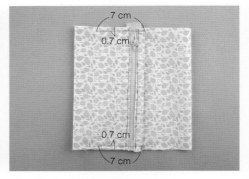

④ The two sides are assembled.

3 SEW THE BOTTOM OF THE POCKET

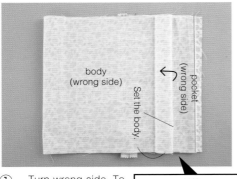

① Turn wrong side. To equalize the width of the body and the pocket, draw the excess line of the pocket.

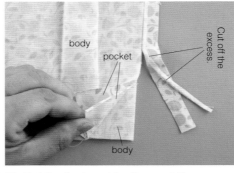

② Set the body aside, then cut the excess from the pocket.

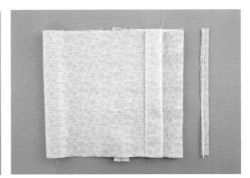

③ The excess of the pocket is cut.

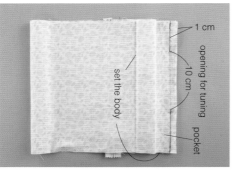

④ Set the body aside. Leave the zipper open. Mark 1 cm from the bottom of the pocket, then sew leaving an opening for turning.

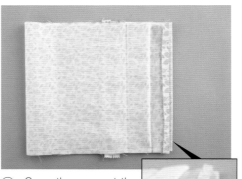

⑤ Open the seam at the bottom of the pocket.

4 SEW THE SIDES

① Replace the body of the pocket, then mark 1 cm from the sides.

② Sew the sides.

③ Cut the corners of the margins.

④ Cut off the excess from the zipper.

⑤ Open the side seam.

⑥ Turn right side out.

5 CLOSE THE OPENING

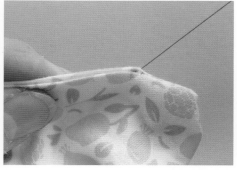

① Make a knot and pull out the needle through the fold at the top edge of the opening.

② Insert the needle into the fold at the bottom edge and take it out 0.2 or 0.3 cm further.

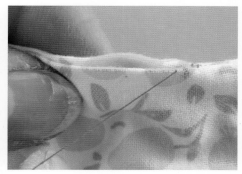

③ Pull the thread.

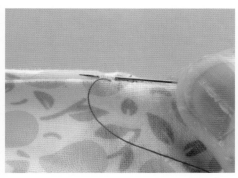

④ Insert the needle into the fold at the top edge and pull it out 0.2 to 0.3 cm further.

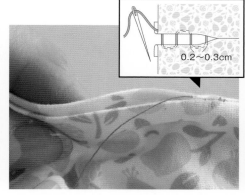

0.2~0.3cm

⑤ Pull the thread. Repeat steps ② to ⑤ to close the opening.

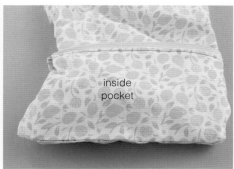

inside pocket

⑥ The opening for turning is closed.

6 FINISH

① Turn the pocket right side out.

outside pocket

② Shape the corners, then iron.

outside pocket

③ The pocket is turned right side out.

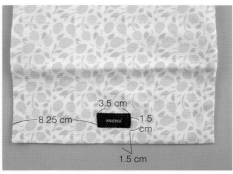

3.5 cm
8.25 cm
1.5 cm
1.5 cm

④ Fold the sides of the label 0.5 cm, then sew it onto the body of the wallet.

COMPLETED!

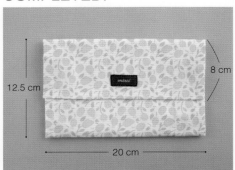

12.5 cm
8 cm
20 cm

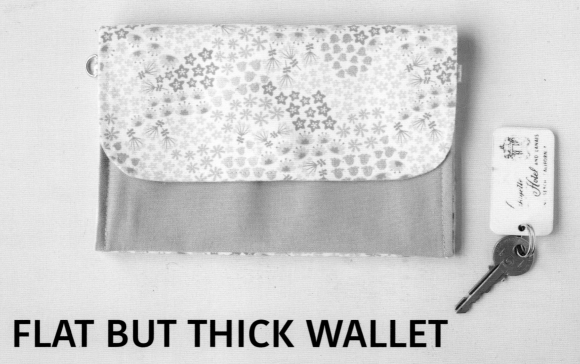

2 FLAT BUT THICK WALLET

Fold the fabric like origami and stitch to make,
this flat wallet. You will see, it is very handy!

Wow!

https://youtu.be/mQ6xhUUfvjE

Instructions: P. 52

Difficulty : ★★☆☆☆

ere are three compartments.

Nice capacity!

The wallet consists of two assembled pockets.

Can be used as a clutch.

is also worn over the shoulder.

A card holder is added inside.

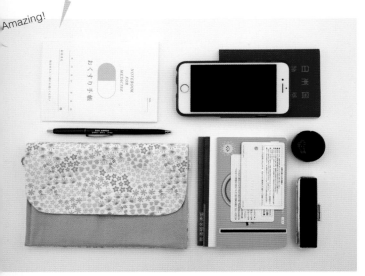

Amazing!

ll these objects can fit in this wallet.

Sew a magnetic button at the end of construction.

3 BAG WITH ORIGINAL AND CLEVER HANDLES

The body of the bag is sewn in a straight line. Insert the handles into the opening of the bag and sew them at the end. The handles create folds and give an original shape to this bag.

https://youtu.be/IQHDOPXQPRc

Instructions: P. 54

14

The seam of the handles forms folds on the opening of the bag.

All seams are made in a straight line.

Insert the handles at the end and sew.

A pocket is added inside.

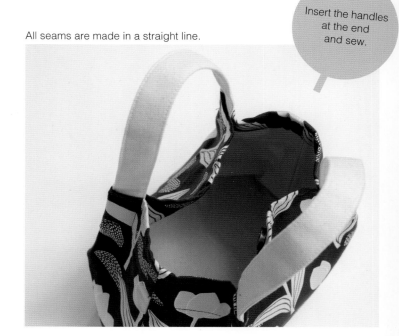

a

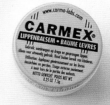

b

4 POUCHES WITH POCKET

At first glance, this pouche seems simple but several pockets are hidden there! The margins are not visible inside the cover. The model a is made of waxed canvas, and the model b is made of simple cotton.

https://youtu.be/WwbX6jttwio

Instructions: P. 56

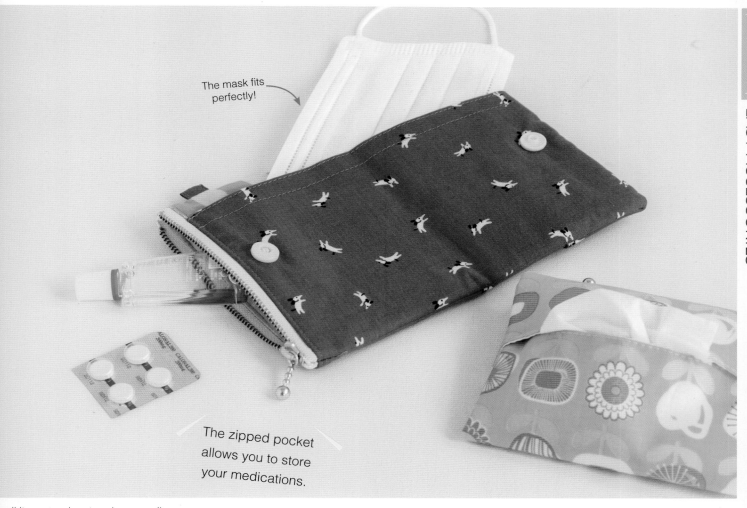

The mask fits perfectly!

The zipped pocket allows you to store your medications.

...mall items can be stored very easily.

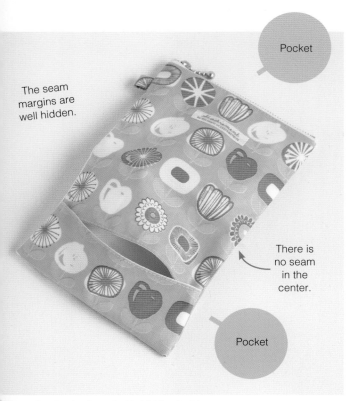

Pocket

The seam margins are well hidden.

There is no seam in the center.

Pocket

...ttle sewing to do. A pocket is hidden inside.

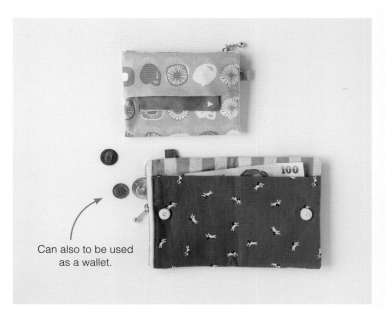

Can also to be used as a wallet.

Put your notes in the large pocket and coins in the zipped pocket. Store your cards in the inside pocket.

5 SMART WALLET

The structure of this wallet is very simple and the pockets can be opened wide to easily access your cards.

Difficulty : ★★⯪☆☆

The partitions of the large pockets open crosswise.

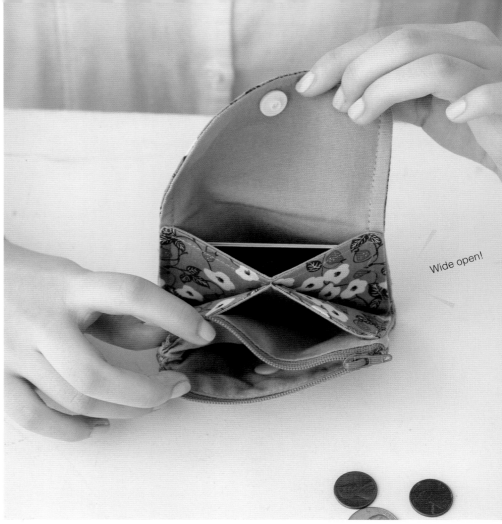

Wide open!

Put your cards in the compartments and coins in the zipped pocket. All compartments widen.

https://youtu.be/bGyb92hZxzs

Instructions: P. 58

CHAPTER 2

CLEVER BAGS AND WALLETS

Models of original form and composition are gathered in this chapter. Not only they are charming but also very practical! Discover very clever designs.

6 TRAPEZOIDAL BOSTON MINI BAGS

A large pocket makes it easy to store things in this bag. Made of quilted fabric, it's very soft and fluffy to the touch!

https://youtu.be/40O2w-h5hNY

Instructions: P. 60

a

b

Its shape is
lovely.

Even a large wallet
can fit in this bag.

Very
practical
large
pocket

Put your passport and
your phone in the outside pocket.

7 MULTIPOCKET YOKE BAGS

Pockets are integrated between the yoke and the outside of the bag. It can be used every day, perhaps to carry your lunch.

https://youtu.be/hiunJ13QMNo

Instructions: P. 63

a

b

Large pockets!

Put a wallet in the pocket
provided for this purpose.

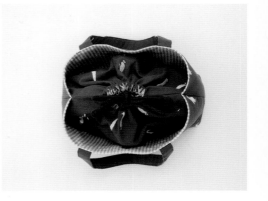

Pockets surround
the inner pouch.

A large wallet
can fit in
the pocket.

Two interior
pockets have
been added.

2 in 1!

Store the pouch
inside the bag
to make it a very
classic tote bag.

8 BELLOWS WALLET & BAG

This bag will be admired by your friends. It is quite simple seen from the outside but the interior is very original. Add a handle to carry it by hand.

Instructions : P. 36

https://youtu.be/7Ids-wAV6w0

a

b

Two models of different sizes are intended, one for essential objects, the other for small toiletries objects.

How?

The three pockets are made with different fabrics.

The bottom of the central pocket is raised.

t is possible to choose various fabrics for he three pockets.

The handle is removable.

The shape is rounded.

Wow!

CONSTRUCTION OF THE BELLOWS WALLET & BAG
NO 8 PAGE 24

Full size patterns in the Pattern Sheet A SIDE

Body, front lining, back lining, flap, flap lining, inside pocket

SUPPLIES (a)

40 x 50 cm of pink Oxford (fabric A)
30 x 45 cm of flowered cotton (fabric B)
30 x 30 cm of cotton with small flowers (fabric C)
50 x 94 cm of iron-on canvas 1 zipper 20 cm long
2 D-rings 1.5 cm wide
1 magnetic button to sew ø 1.8 cm
1 leather handle 20 cm long with carabiners

SUPPLIES (b)

30 x 45 cm of pink Oxford (fabric A)
25 x 40 cm of flowered cotton (fabric B)
25 x 25 cm of cotton with small flowers (fabric C)
30 x 94 cm of iron-on canvas
1 zipper 20 cm long
2 D-rings 1 cm wide
1 magnetic button to sew ø 1.8 cm
1 leather handle 20 cm long with carabiners

Cutting Plan

※ Trace the tab directly on the fabric.
※ ☐ The numbers in the squares correspond to the seam allowances.
※ Add a 1 cm margin, unless otherwise indicated.
※ Heat the pieces indicated in blue.

> Read the two digits:
> **Top Digit:** model a
> **Bottom Digit:** model b

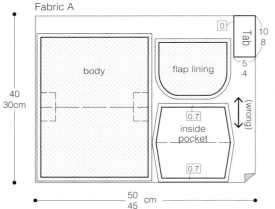

Fabric A

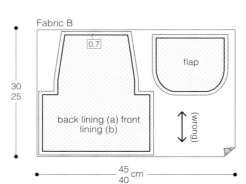

Fabric B

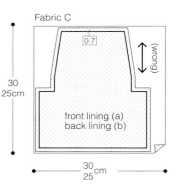

Fabric C

PREPARATION

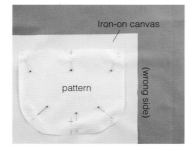

① Heat the wrong side of the fabric (see p. 49). Pin the pattern onto the iron-on fabric.

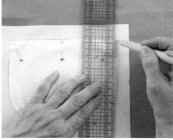

② Trace the pattern using a ruler and a marker.

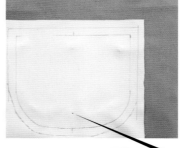

③ Add a seam margin. Drill a hole at the location of the magnetic button.

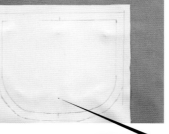

④ Cut the fabric.

THE INSTRUCTIONS ARE FOR MODEL A

1 SEW THE ZIPPER AND MAKE THE INSIDE POCKET

※ A different thread colour is used here for better visibility.

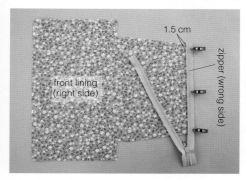

① Place the zipper on the edge of the front lining, right sides together. Hold with clips.

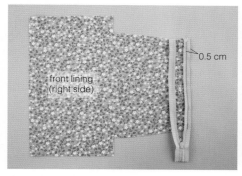

② Stitch 0.5 cm from the edge.

③ Place the inner pocket on the edge of the front lining, right sides together. Sew 0.7 cm from the edge.

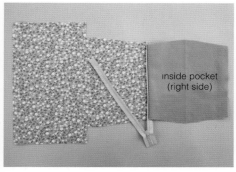

④ Fold the inside pocket right side out.

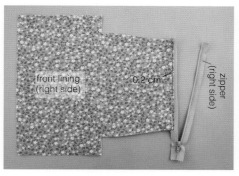

⑤ Fold the inside pocket over the back of the front lining. Topstitch 0.2 cm from the zipper.

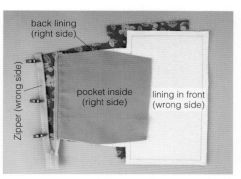

⑥ Place the zipper on the edge of the back lining, right sides together. Hold with clips.

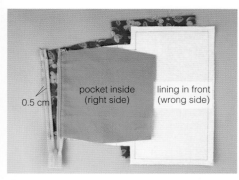

⑦ Sew 0.5 cm from the edge.

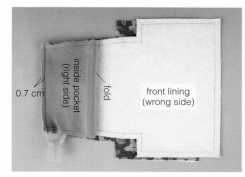

⑧ Fold the inner pocket in half, right sides together, and align with the zipper. Sew 0.7 cm from the edge.

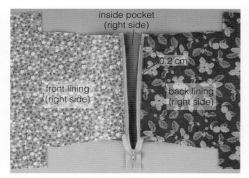

⑨ Turn right side out. Topstitch 0.2 cm from the zipper.

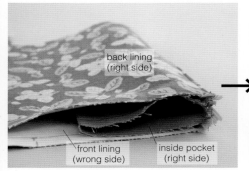

⑩ Overlap the back lining, the inside pocket and the front lining, then hold the assembly with clips.

⑪ Sew 0.7 cm from the sides to assemble the inner pocket.

2 SEW THE BELLOWS OF THE LINING

① Match the marks ☆ on the back lining, then pin.

② Line up the ☆ marks on the front lining, then pin.

③ Sew each lining up to the mark ☆.

3 SEW THE SIDES OF THE LINING

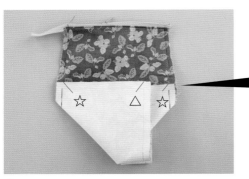

④ Sew the other bellows up to the ☆ mark in the same way.

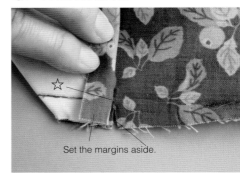

① Set the bellow margin aside from the back lining and notch the edge of one piece.

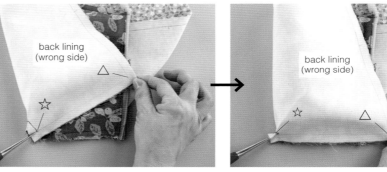

② Set the bellow margin aside from the front lining and notch the edge of one piece.

③ Hold the opening of the bag (△) with your fingers Place the awl on the ☆ mark. Then align the side of the back lining.

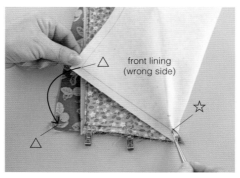

④ Hold the side with clips.

⑤ Hold the opening of the front (△) with your fingers. Place the awl on the ☆ mark, then align the other side of the back lining.

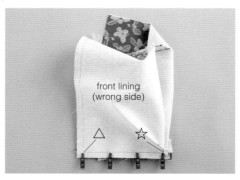

⑥ Hold the assembly with clips.

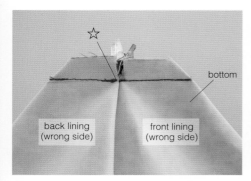

⑦ Bottom view. Match the marks ☆.

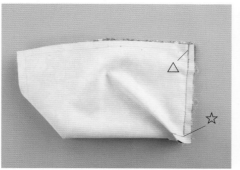

⑧ Sew each lining up to the mark ☆.

⑨ Open the side seam.

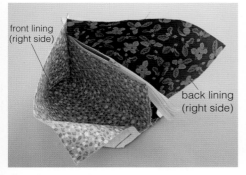

⑩ One side of the lining is sewn.

⑪ Sew the other side of the lining in the same way.

⑫ Cut off the excess from the zipper. Open the side seam.

4 MAKE THE FLAP

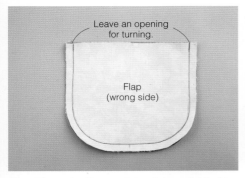

① Place the flap and the lining, right sides together. Sew the outline leaving an opening for turning.

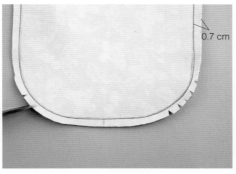

② Equalize the margins to 0.7 cm from the seam. Notching the margins of the curve.

③ Open the seam.

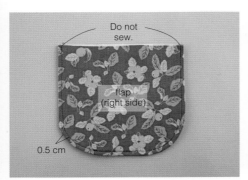

④ Turn right side out. Topstitch 0.5 cm from the edge.

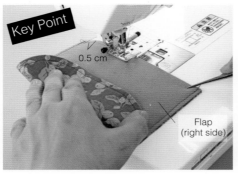

⑤ Fold the flap over to the lining to provide some comfort. Stitch the opening 0.5 cm from the edge.

⑥ The flap is naturally curved.

5 SEW THE SIDES OF THE LINING

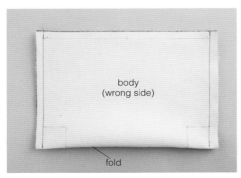

① Fold the body in half, right sides together, then sew the sides.

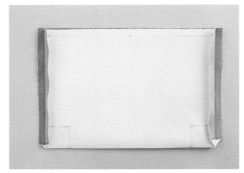

② Open the seam.

7 SEW THE TAB

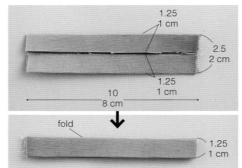

① Fold the edges of the tab towards the middle, then fold in half. ※ The top measurement corresponds to model a and the bottom measurement to model b.

② Cut the excess 1 cm from the seam.

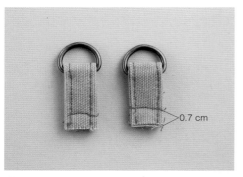

③ Pass the tab through the D ring and fold in 2 half. Sew 0.5 cm from the edge.

8 SEW THE FLAP

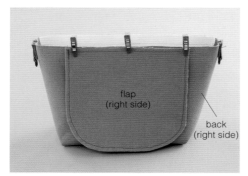

① Hold the flap on the back with clips.

④ Turn right side out. Place the legs on the sides and hold with clips.

② Sew 0.9 cm from the edge to assemble.

6 SEW THE BELLOWS

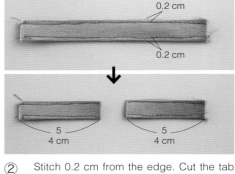

① Line up the side and the bottom center, then sew the bellow. ※ The top measurement corresponds to model a and the bottom measurement to model b.

② Stitch 0.2 cm from the edge. Cut the tab in 2 parts.

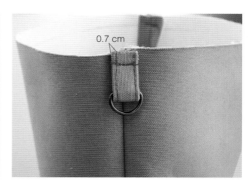

⑤ Sew 0.7 cm from the edge to assemble.

9 SEW THE OPENING OF THE BAG

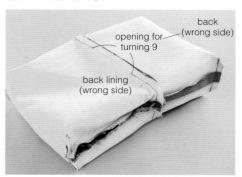

① Make the opening of the bag and the lining line up. Sew leaving a 9 cm opening for turning.

② Open the seam of the opening of the bag.

③ Turn right side out.

Sew

④ Close the opening (see p. 93).

9 SEW THE MAGNETIC BUTTON

0.3 cm

⑤ Topstitch the opening of the bag 0.3 cm from the edge.

Flap lining (right side)

① Place the magnetic button (凸) on the back of the flap, then mark the four corners.

② Make one stop knot. Insert the needle in the center of the location of the magnetic button and pull it out at an angle, pricking only the lining.

③ Place the magnetic button (凸), then take the needle out through the corner hole. Insert the needle into the lining and take it out through the hole.

④ Pass the needle through the loop.

⑤ Pull the thread.

COMPLETED!

⑥ Make three stitches in each hole. The magnetic button (凸) is sewn.

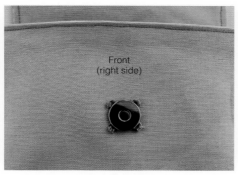

Front (right side)

⑦ Sew the other magnetic button (凹) in the same way on the front.

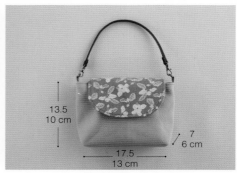

13.5
10 cm

7
6 cm

17.5
13 cm

⑧ Attach the handle in the rings D.
※ The top measurement corresponds to model a and the bottom measurement to model.

 MULTIPOCKET FLAT BAG

The model p.24 is transformed here
into a flat bag, easier to make.

Instructions : P. 66

https://youtu.be/WPP_4G7j0C8

Two models, two levels of difficulty.

Advanced level   Easy level

The composition of the pieces is identical for the two models. Without bellows, the kit is easier to make than the bag.

Interior view. The kit is fully lined.

Surprising

ou can use three different fabrics for each compartment.

Keep your toiletries.

Also use this kit as a card holder.

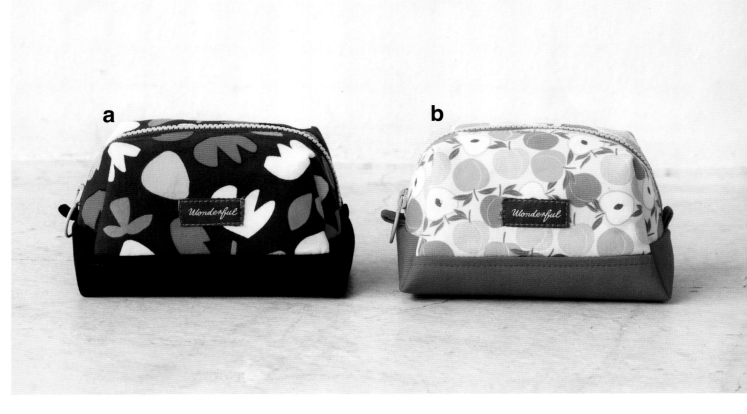

Difficulty: ★★★☆☆

10 TRAPEZOIDAL POUCHES

The shape of these models is original.
Combine two fabrics of your choice.

This trapezodial form is original!

Instructions: P. 68

https://youtu.be/Wh1TvwTAKp8

A fabric with large patterns and a plain fabric blend perfectly.

Choose a light-colored fabric for the lining.

11 "SHELL" POUCHES

Fold the body of the case in half and add a zipper. The shape of these pouches is reminiscent of a shell.

Difficulty: ★★★☆☆

a

b

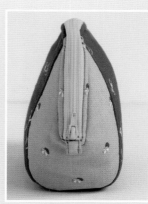

Side view

c

Instructions: P.70

https://youtu.be/5BiW6Pd5ITw

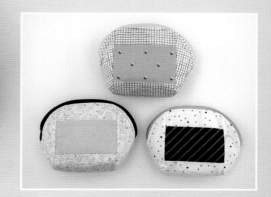

Inside out pouches.
A small pocket is added.

12
BAG WITH ROUNDED OPENING

The bag opening is rounded. Put valuables in the two zipped pockets and those you use often in the middle of the bag.

Difficulty: ★★★★★

https://youtu.be/rg2JSisHIWE
Instructions : P. 74

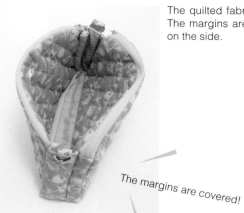

The quilted fabric protects your objects. The margins are covered with the fabric on the side.

The margins are covered!

Easy to use!

The left pocket is embossed so that you can slip a large object into it.

Put your phone in the middle of the bag.

faire a la main
Today is happy day

13 MULTIPOCKET TOTE

Difficulty: ★★★☆☆

Six pockets surround the body of the bag.
This helps organize your storage.

a

b

Very practical!

The side pocket is perfect for carrying your phone.

A bottle holder is integrated.

The bottom comes up 2 cm to keep the shape of the bag.

Instructions: P. 78

https://youtu.be/s6DIk1gyGbQ

CHAPTER 3

CLEVER AND PRACTICAL ACCESSORIES

The models in this chapter will help organize your home. Discover decorative items, pencil cases and other interesting ideas!

14 VANITY CASE

Instructions: P. 81

https://youtu.be/ND5x-Imvaaw

PART 3

Difficulty: ★★☆☆☆

Tighten the opening of this bag to carry all your toiletries.

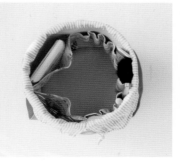

It has two large compartments and ten small ones.

Place the yoke outside to better see the objects stored inside.

Easy to find.

41

15 STORAGE BOXES

Pens, sewing or knitting equipment, kitchen utensils can be stored in these pretty fabric boxes. These boxes are the favorites of my Instagram community.

a: Instructions: P. 84

a   https://youtu.be/uVt_ZI9GEZs

b: Instructions: P. 86

b   https://youtu.be/1JBEbSdPgPU

Mega capacity!

The handle is removable.

You can hang it on the handle of a closet.

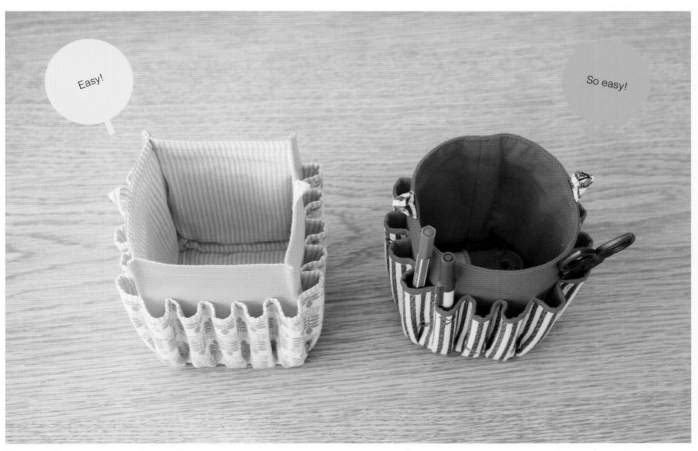

Easy!

So easy!

Start with the square model, it is easier to achieve.

THREE USES OF METAL REINFORCEMENTS

Metal frames are often used to open sleeves.
Three original ideas are proposed here.

The 15 cm wide reinforcements are used here.

16 WALLET WITH A TAB

Easy to achieve!

Difficulty: ★☆☆☆☆

Instructions: P. 88

https://youtu.be/2oq76pPc-Qw

The sleeve can be opened widely.

Simply sew a press stud.

Sleeves with metal reinforcements often have a zipper.
But here, the closure is replaced by a tab, to facilitate its construction.

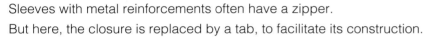

17 MINI BAG

Difficulty: ★☆☆☆☆

Use the metal reinforcements as handles. Store your essentials to go shopping!

Instructions : P. 90

https://youtu.be/4pMobZ-H3hY

The handles are solid!

44

18 WALL STORAGE BOXES

Difficulty: ★★☆☆☆

a

The reinforcement serves as the opening!

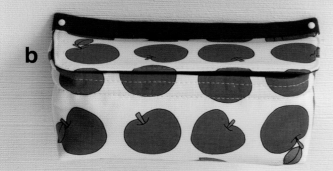

b

Use the metal reinforcements horizontally to make these rectangular storage boxes that you can pin on a wall.

c

Perfect for storing sewing threads and masking tape.

Instructions : P. 92

https://youtu.be/y4d5TsCcaA0

19 PENCIL CASES

Pull the handle to very easily open these kits.
They hold perfectly, placed on a table.

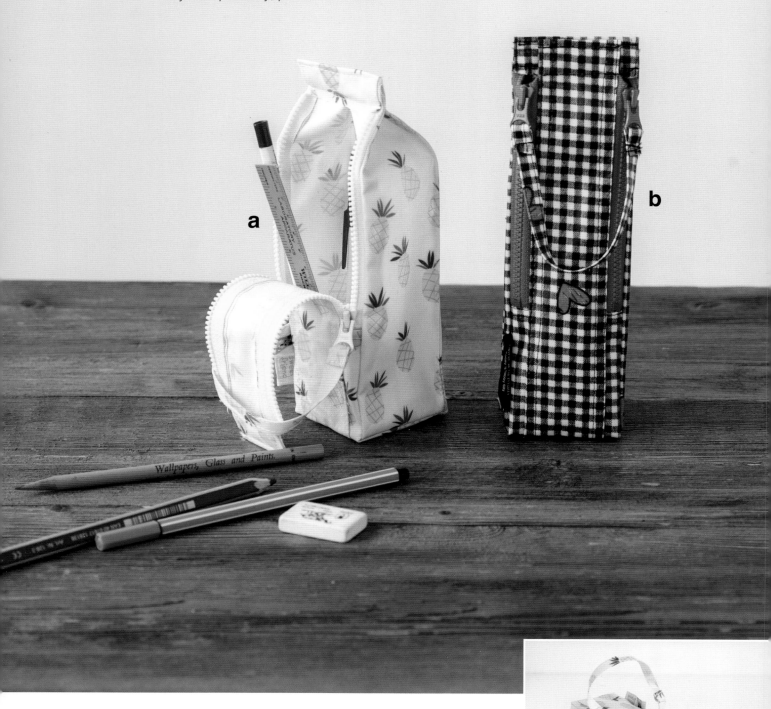

a

b

Instructions: P.94

https://youtu.be/v0QqE4c-Pyk

A magnetic button is inserted
under the opening.

46

Easy opening!

Easy to take out!

The case stands.

EQUIPMENT AND SUPPLIES

TISSIE PAPER
The tissue paper is semi transparent and is used to transfer the patterns to full size.

WEIGHT
To keep the paper in place when transferring patterns.

RULE
To measure, draw the lines and add seam margins. A transparent Omnigrid rule is practical.

MARKERS
To put marks on the fabric. There are several types: air erasable (a), water erasable (b), mechanical pencil (c).

TAILOR'S SCISSORS
To cut the fabric. Never cut paper with this type of scissors.

THREAD SNIPPERS
To cut the thread and the delicate parts.

AWL
To punch through the fabric and shape the corners.

PINS
To hold more than two fabrics.

CLIPS
To hold more than two fabrics on which the needle holes may be visible.

SEWING THREAD N°60
To sew. Choose needles nos 80 to 100 depending on the thickness of the fabrics.

ADHESIVE TAPE
To maintain waxed fabrics. Glue on the sewing machine plate as a guide.

PATTERN CONSTRUCTION

Carry-over of patterns in real size

※ Add seam margins following the cutting plane.
※ The unit of measurement is the centimeter.

① Put tissue paper on the insert, then put weights to hold it together.

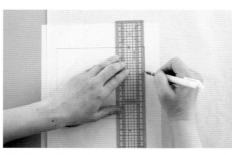

② Trace the pattern using a ruler and a pencil.

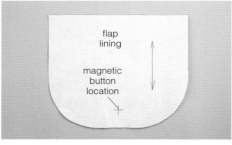

flap lining

magnetic button location

③ Also trace marks and straight wire. Cut the pattern.

Legend of lines and symbols

Finishing Line	Mark	Fold
——	— —	— — —
* Straight-wire *	Fold Line	Seam line
←——→	— —— —	-------------
Magnetic Button	Fold Direction	
+	b ///// a ➡	b\ a

※ Straight-Wire: Direction parallel to warp threads

Cutting plane

Fold the fabric in half, right sides together, then place the pattern on the fabric, making the fold of the fabric coincide with the edge indicated

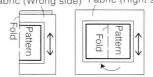

Fabric (Wrong side)   Fabric (Right side)

Pattern with "fold"

Place the patterns on the fabric following the cutting plane. Add seam margins, then cut the pieces. The rectangular pieces have no pattern, trace them directly on the fabric.

Fabric (Wrong side)   Fabric (Right side)

FUSIBLE FABRIC

Types of fusible fabric

This canvas is glued to the back of the fabric using an iron to prevent deformation of the work and to consolidate the fabric.

Fusible fleece

One side of the fleece is coated with glue. The appearance is soft and fluffy.

thick

Thick fusible fabric

medium

Medium fusible fabric

thin

Thin fusible fabric

Fusible fabric fixing

Put the sticky side of the fusible fabric against the back of the fabric. Place a weight and squeeze the iron without sliding it.

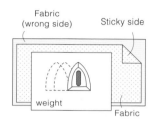

Fabric (wrong side)　Sticky side

weight

Fabric

Fusible fleece fixing

Lay the sticky side of the fusible fleece against the back of the fabric. Turn the fabric over, then press the iron to the right side of the fabric without sliding it.

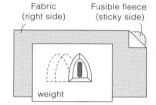

Fabric (right side)　Fusible fleece (sticky side)

weight

MACHINE SEWING

● Start and end of the seam

Sew two or three points back and forth to consolidate the beginning and the end of the seam.

0.5 to 1 cm stop point

(wrong side)

(wrong side)

Poke 2 or 3

● Sewing an angle

Sew one corner stitch at an angle to obtain a sharp angle.

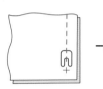 →  →

Stitch up to one point on the corner. Leave the needle in the fabric, raise the foot, then turn the fabric.

Lower the foot and make one stitch at an angle.

Leave the needle in the fabric, raise the foot, then turn the fabric.

KEY POINT

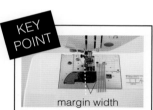

margin width

If there is no guide on the machine plate, measure the distance from the needle, then tape the distance to the seam margin.

OIL CLOTH

Cut

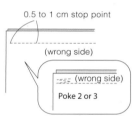

pattern

(wrong side)

The needle holes are visible on the fabric, so do not use pins. Apply weights to maintain the pattern. Glue the corner with adhesive tape.

Seam The standard foot does not slide easily on the oilcloth. Use a teflon foot or nylon tape to facilitate sewing.

Teflon foot
This foot slides easily on the oilcloth.

or

Nylon tape　Recommended

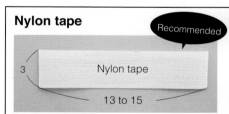

3

Nylon tape

13 to 15

Cut 13 to 15 cm of 3 cm wide nylon tape and slip this tape under the presser foot.

KEY POINT

It is also convenient for sewing quilted fabric.

● Use of nylon tape

① Hold the fabric with clips.

② Place the nylon tape under the foot, then stitch.

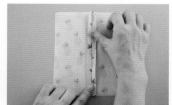

③ Open the seam.

④ Place the nylon tape under the foot, then topstitch.

KEY POINTS

MAGNETIC BUTTON FIXING NO 3 PAGE 14

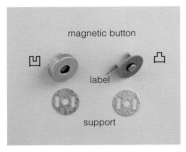 

This magnetic button consists of four pieces.

① Put the mark of the magnetic button on the right side of the cloth.

② Place the support on the mark, then mark the label.

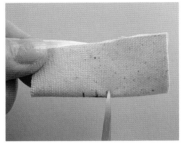  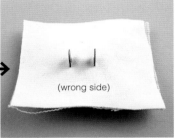

③ Fold the fabric in 2, then cut the marks.

④ Insert the label of the magnetic button.

⑤ Add the support.

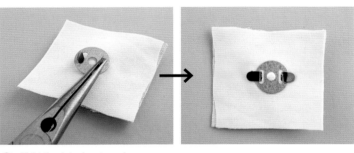 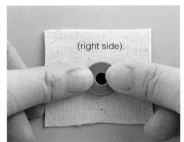 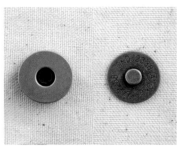

⑥ Fold the label outward.

⑦ Turn the fabric on the right side. Press the button against a table to fold down completely the labels.

⑧ Fix the other magnetic button in the same way.

METAL REINFORCEMENTS INSERTION

NO 16 PAGE 44   NO 17 PAGE 44   NO 18 PAGE 45

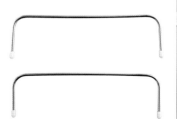   

Prepare the 5 x 15 cm metal reinforcements.

① Insert the metal reinforcement in the slide.

② Insert to the other end.

③ The two frames are inserted behind the slides

50

PLASTIC PUSH-BUTTON FIXING

NO 4 PAGE 16 **NO 5 PAGE 18** **NO 7 PAGE 22** **NO 12 PAGE 36**

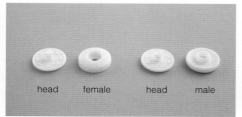

head   female   head   male

The push-button consists of four pieces. Most push-buttons require the use of pliers.

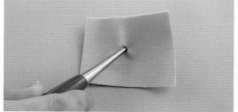

① Drill a hole at the location of the push-button.

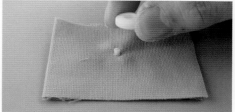

② Insert the head into the back of the fabric. Place the female part on the right side of the fabric.

Female   Head

③ Press the two pieces together. (Use special pliers for this procedure.)

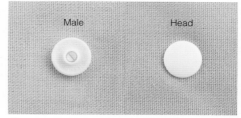

Male   Head

④ Fix the male push-button in the same way.

ON THE OIL CLOTH

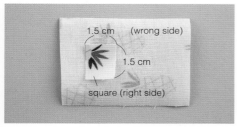

1.5 cm   (wrong side)

1.5 cm

square (right side)

① Place a 1.5 x 1.5 cm square of fabric on the back of the fabric.

② Drill the hole in the two fabrics.

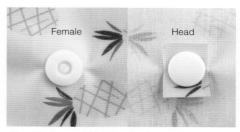

Female   Head

③ Fix the push-button as shown above.

HIDDEN MAGNET **NO 19 PAGE 46**

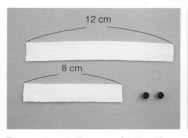

12 cm

8 cm

Prepare two twill tapes of 1.5 x 12 cm and 1.5 x 8 cm and one pair of magnets.

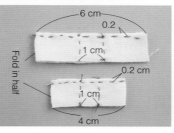

6 cm

0.2

1 cm

0.2 cm

Fold in half

1 cm

4 cm

① Fold the tapes in half, then sew as shown in the photo.

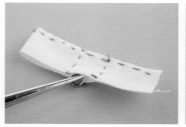

② Insert the magnet in the middle of the tape.

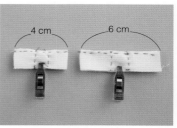

4 cm   6 cm

③ Hold the opening with clips.

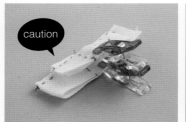

caution

④ Overlap the two tapes to check if the magnets match.

⑤ Make the marks.

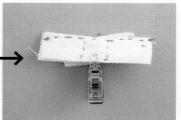

Insert the tape with the magnet.

⑥ Place the face with the mark on the reverse side of the work, then sew.
※ For more details, see P. 95.

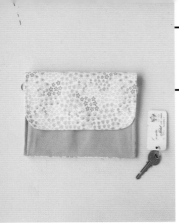

FLAT BUT THICK WALLET

NO 2 PAGE 12

SUPPLIES

40 x 40 cm of cotton with flowers (fabric A)
25 x 30 cm of Oxford plain mauve (fabric B)
40 x 50 cm of printed cotton (fabric C)
40 x 50 cm of fusible fabric
2 D rings
1 magnetic button to sew ø 1.8 cm

PREPARATION

Heat-seal bodies A and B.

※ Trace body B, the lining of body B, the tab and the pocket directly on the fabric.
※ The numbers in the square correspond to the seam margins. Add 1 cm margin, unless otherwise indicate
※ Heat-seal the blue parts.

Cutting Plans

Fabric A
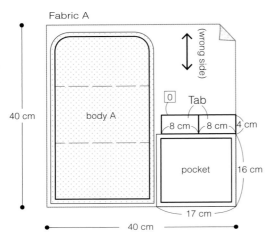

Fabric B
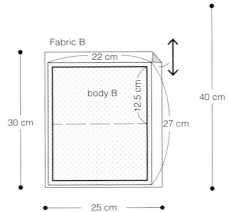

Fabric C
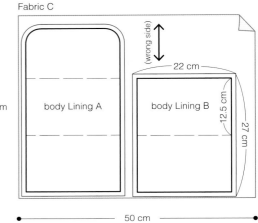

CONSTRUCTION

1 MAKE THE POCKET

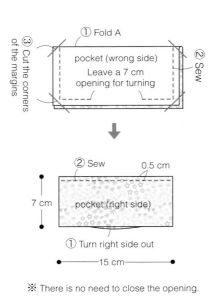

※ There is no need to close the opening.

2 MAKE BODY A

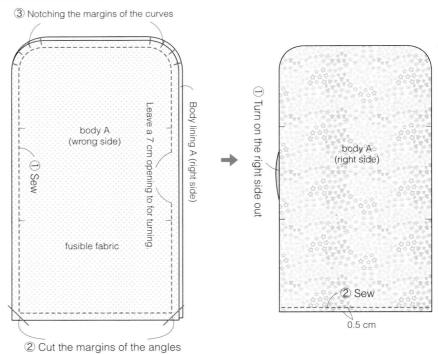

52

3 MAKE BODY B

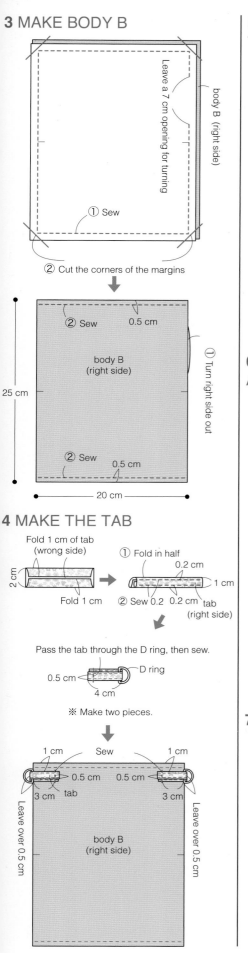

Leave a 7 cm opening for turning

body B (right side)

① Sew

② Cut the corners of the margins

② Sew   0.5 cm

body B (right side)

① Turn right side out

25 cm

② Sew   0.5 cm

20 cm

4 MAKE THE TAB

Fold 1 cm of tab (wrong side)

2 cm

Fold 1 cm

① Fold in half

0.2 cm

1 cm

② Sew 0.2   0.2 cm   tab (right side)

Pass the tab through the D ring, then sew.

0.5 cm

D ring

4 cm

※ Make two pieces.

1 cm   Sew   1 cm

0.5 cm   0.5 cm

3 cm   tab   3 cm

Leave over 0.5 cm   Leave over 0.5 cm

body B (right side)

5 SEW THE POCKET ON THE LINING

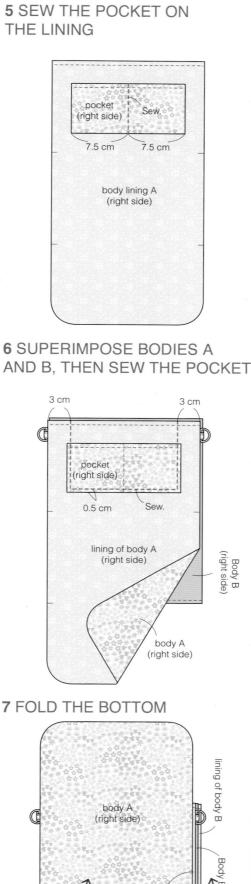

pocket (right side)   Sew.

7.5 cm   7.5 cm

body lining A (right side)

6 SUPERIMPOSE BODIES A AND B, THEN SEW THE POCKET

3 cm   3 cm

pocket (right side)

0.5 cm   Sew.

lining of body A (right side)

Body B (right side)

body A (right side)

7 FOLD THE BOTTOM

lining of body B

body A (right side)

Body B

② Fold   body lining A   ① Fold

8 SEW THE SIDES OF BODY B

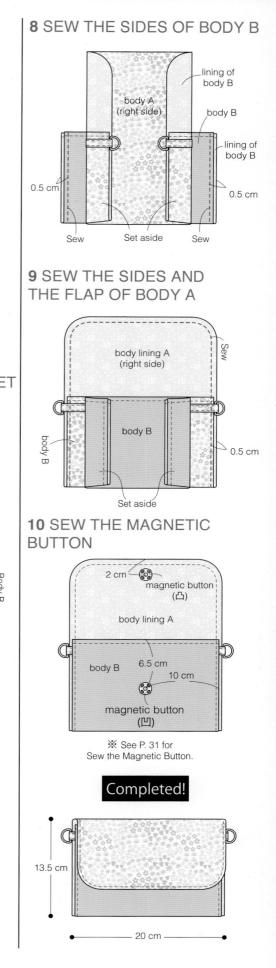

lining of body B

body A (right side)

body B

lining of body B

0.5 cm   0.5 cm

Sew   Set aside   Sew

9 SEW THE SIDES AND THE FLAP OF BODY A

body lining A (right side)

Sew

body B   body B

0.5 cm

Set aside

10 SEW THE MAGNETIC BUTTON

2 cm   magnetic button (凸)

body lining A

body B   6.5 cm   10 cm

magnetic button (凹)

※ See P. 31 for Sew the Magnetic Button.

Completed!

13.5 cm

20 cm

53

BAG WITH ORIGINAL AND CLEVER HANDLES

NO 3 PAGE 14

SUPPLIES

35 x 110 cm of printed Oxford (fabric A)
70 x 110 cm of unbleached plain Oxford (fabric B)
60 x 94 cm of fusible fabric
1 magnetic button ø 1.8 cm

PREPARATION

Heat the body and the bottom.

Cutting Plans

※ There is no pattern for this model.
Trace all the pieces directly on the fabric.
※ The numbers in the square correspond to the seam margins.
Add 1 cm margin, unless otherwise indicated.
※ Heat-seal the blue parts.

Fabric A

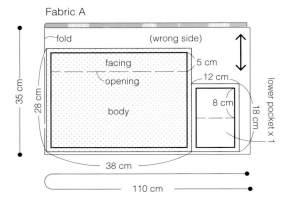

Fabric B

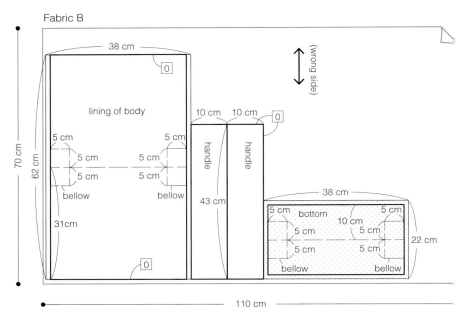

CONSTRUCTION

1 HEAT THE BODY AND THE BOTTOM

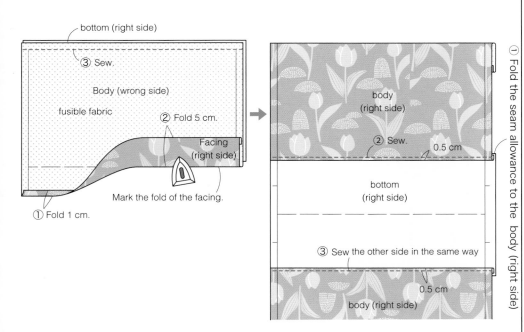

2 SEW THE SIDES

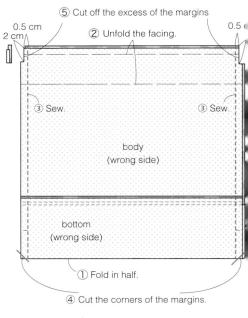

3 SEW THE BELLOWS

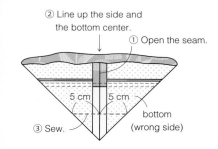

② Line up the side and the bottom center.
① Open the seam.
5 cm 5 cm
③ Sew.
bottom (wrong side)

4 SEW THE POCKET ON THE LINING.

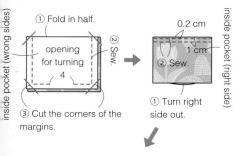

① Fold in half.
inside pocket (wrong sides)
opening for turning 4
② Sew.
③ Cut the corners of the margins.

0.2 cm
1 cm
② Sew.
inside pocket (right side)
① Turn right side out.

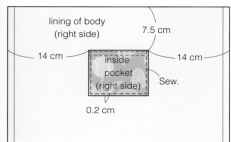

lining of body (right side)
7.5 cm
14 cm
inside pocket (right side)
Sew.
14 cm
0.2 cm

5 SEW THE SIDES OF THE LINING

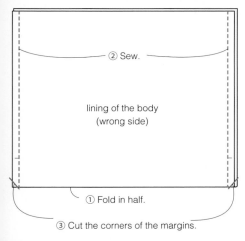

② Sew.
lining of the body (wrong side)
① Fold in half.
③ Cut the corners of the margins.

6 SEW THE BELLOWS OF THE LINING

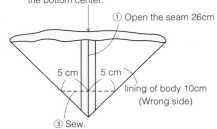

② Line up the side and the bottom center.
① Open the seam 26cm
5 cm 5 cm
lining of body 10cm (Wrong side)
③ Sew.

7 SEW THE MARGINS OF THE BELLOWS OF THE BODY AND THE LINING

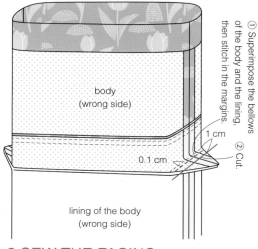

body (wrong side)
① Superimpose the bellows of the body and the lining, then stitch in the margins.
② Cut.
1 cm
0.1 cm
lining of the body (wrong side)

8 SEW THE FACING

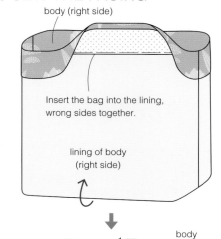

body (right side)
Insert the bag into the lining, wrong sides together.
lining of body (right side)

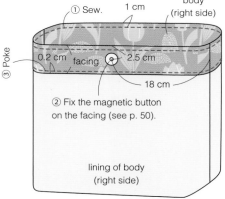

① Sew.
1 cm
body (right side)
③ Poke
0.2 cm facing 2.5 cm
18 cm
② Fix the magnetic button on the facing (see p. 50).
lining of body (right side)

9 MAKE THE HANDLES

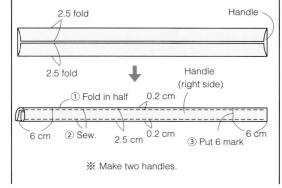

2.5 fold
Handle
2.5 fold
Handle (right side)
① Fold in half. 0.2 cm
6 cm ② Sew. 2.5 cm 0.2 cm 6 cm
③ Put 6 mark
※ Make two handles.

10 SEW THE HANDLES

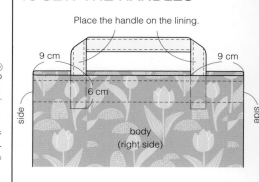

Place the handle on the lining.
9 cm 6 cm 9 cm
epis
body (right side)
side

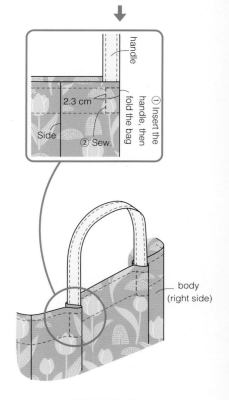

handle
2.3 cm
Side
① Insert the handle, then fold the bag.
② Sew.

body (right side)

Completed!

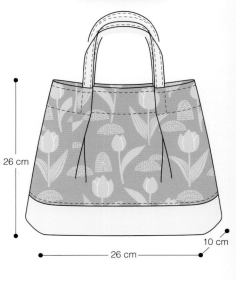

26 cm
26 cm
10 cm

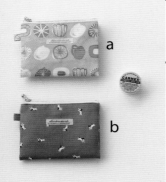

POUCHES WITH POCKET

NO 4 PAGE 16

SUPPLIES (a)

20 x 50 cm of flower oilcloth (fabric A)
20 x 70 cm of white polyester (fabric B)
1 zipper of 12 cm long
1 push button ø 1.3 cm
1 label of 1 x 5.5 cm

SUPPLIES (b)

30 x 50 cm of printed cotton (fabric A)
20 x 70 cm of striped cotton (fabric B)
20 x 30 cm of fusible fabric
1 zipper of 12 cm long
1 push button ø 1.3 cm
1 label of 1 x 5.5 cm

PREPARATION

Heat-seal bodies A and B (model B).

Cutting Plans

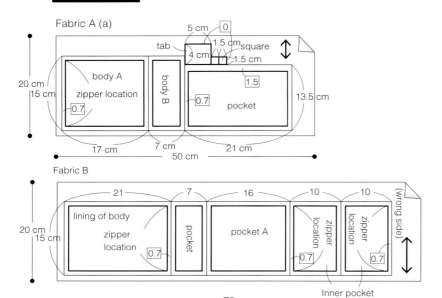

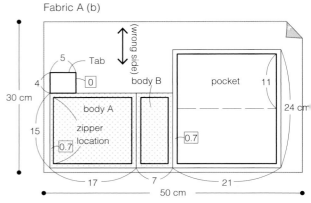

※ There is no pattern for this model.
Trace all the pieces directly on the fabric.
※ The numbers in the square correspond to the seam allowances.
Add 1 cm margin, unless otherwise indicated.
※ Heat-seal the blue parts. ▭

CONSTRUCTION

1 SEW BODY A AND POCKET A

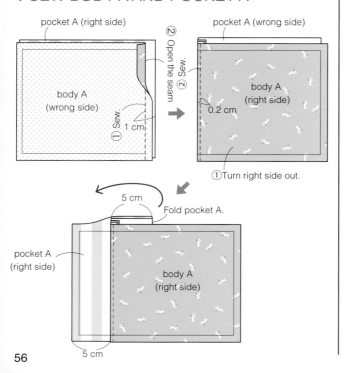

2 SEW BODY B AND POCKET B

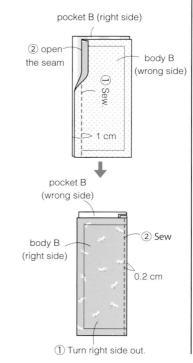

3 SEW BODIES A AND B

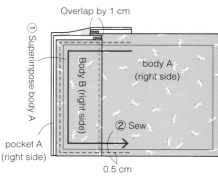

4 SEW THE ZIPPER TO BODY

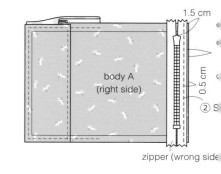

SEW THE TAB

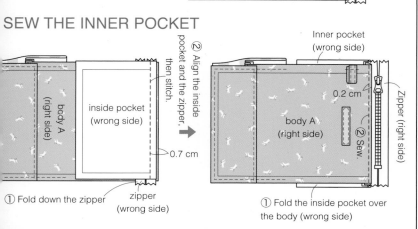

tab (wrong side)
Fold 1 cm
① Fold in half
0.2 cm
1 cm 0.2 cm
Fold 1 cm
tab (right side)
2.5 cm
Fold in half

② Assemble.
0.7 cm 1.5 cm
tab (right side)
Body
label A (right side)
4.5 cm
0.5 fold
① Sew
2.5
0.2 cm
Set the zipper aside
zipper (right side)

SEW THE INNER POCKET

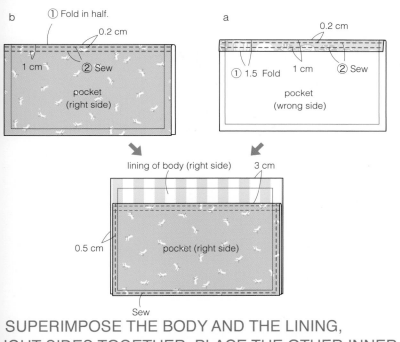

② Align the inside pocket and the zipper, then stitch.
body A (right side)
inside pocket (wrong side)
0.7 cm
① Fold down the zipper
zipper (wrong side)

Inner pocket (wrong side)
0.2 cm
body A (right side)
② Sew.
Zipper (right side)
① Fold the inside pocket over the body (wrong side)

MAKE THE POCKET AND ASSEMBLE IT TO THE LINING

b
① Fold in half.
0.2 cm
1 cm
② Sew
pocket (right side)

a
0.2 cm
① 1.5 Fold
1 cm
② Sew
pocket (wrong side)

lining of body (right side) 3 cm
0.5 cm
pocket (right side)
Sew

SUPERIMPOSE THE BODY AND THE LINING, RIGHT SIDES TOGETHER. PLACE THE OTHER INNER POCKET UNDERNEATH, THEN SEW

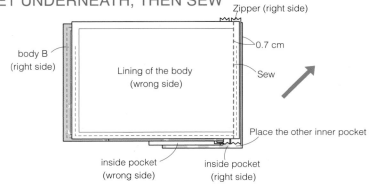

Zipper (right side)
body B (right side)
Lining of the body (wrong side)
0.7 cm
Sew
inside pocket (wrong side)
inside pocket (right side)
Place the other inner pocket

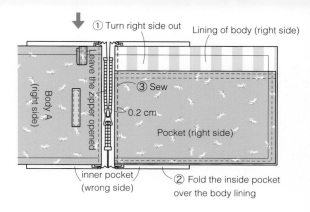

① Turn right side out
Lining of body (right side)
Body A (right side)
Leave the zipper opened
③ Sew
0.2 cm
Pocket (right side)
inner pocket (wrong side)
② Fold the inside pocket over the body lining

9 SEW THE CONTOUR

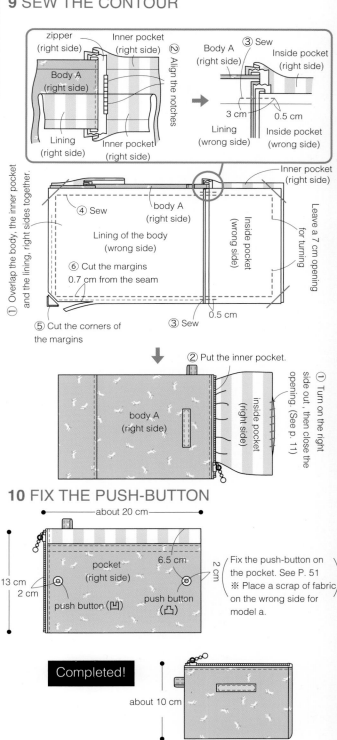

zipper (right side)
Inner pocket (right side)
Body A (right side)
② Align the notches
Lining (right side)
Inner pocket (right side)

Body A (right side)
③ Sew
Inside pocket (right side)
3 cm
0.5 cm
Lining (wrong side)
Inside pocket (wrong side)

Inner pocket (right side)
① Overlap the body, the inner pocket and the lining, right sides together.
④ Sew
body A (right side)
Lining of the body (wrong side)
⑥ Cut the margins 0.7 cm from the seam
Inside pocket (wrong side)
Leave a 7 cm opening for turning
⑤ Cut the corners of the margins
③ Sew
0.5 cm

② Put the inner pocket.
body A (right side)
inside pocket (right side)
① Turn on the right side, then close the opening. (See p. 11)

10 FIX THE PUSH-BUTTON

about 20 cm
13 cm
2 cm
pocket (right side)
6.5 cm
2 cm
push button (凹)
push button (凸)
Fix the push-button on the pocket. See P. 51
※ Place a scrap of fabric on the wrong side for model a.

Completed!
about 10 cm
13 cm

SMART WALLET
NO 5 PAGE 18

(Body, lining of body)

SUPPLIES

30 x 30 cm of flower cotton (fabric A)
30 x 45 cm of gray Oxford (fabric B)
30 x 30 cm of iron-on fabric
1 zipper 15 cm long
1 snap ø 1.3 cm

PREPARATION

Heat-seal the body and the pocket (except the margin).

CONSTRUCTION

1 SEW THE ZIPPER AND THE INSIDE POCKET TO THE BODY

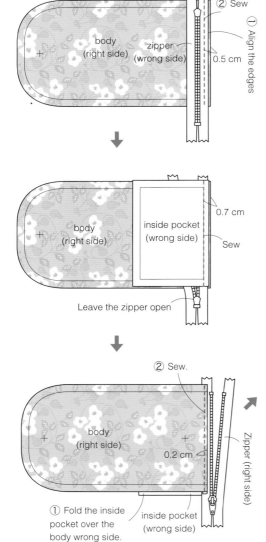

Cutting Plans

※ There is no pattern for the pockets of this model. Trace them directly on the fabric.
※ The numbers in the square correspond to the seam allowances. Add 1 cm margin, unless otherwise indicated.
※ Heat-seal the blue parts.

Fabric A

(wrong side)

30 cm

body

pocket

13

15 cm

0.7

6.5

30 cm

Fabric B

(wrong side)

30 cm

lining of body

pocket lining

13 cm

13 cm

outer pocket   0.7

inner pocket   0.7

0.7

6.5   15

45 cm

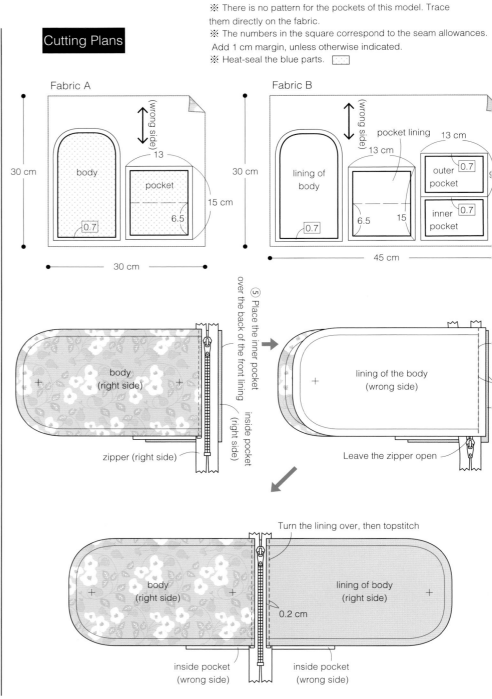

58

SUPERIMPOSE THE BODY AND THE LINING, THE INNER POCKETS, RIGHT SIDES TOGETHER, THEN SEW THE OUTLINE

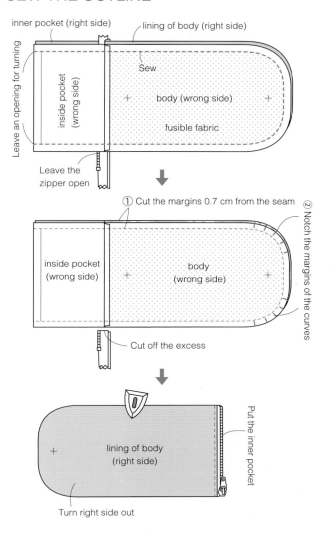

inner pocket (right side)
lining of body (right side)

Leave an opening for turning

inside pocket (wrong side)

Sew

body (wrong side)

fusible fabric

Leave the zipper open

① Cut the margins 0.7 cm from the seam
② Notch the margins of the curves

inside pocket (wrong side)

body (wrong side)

Cut off the excess

lining of body (right side)

Put the inner pocket

Turn right side out

MAKE THE POCKET

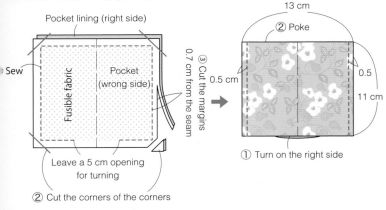

Pocket lining (right side)

Sew

Fusible fabric

Pocket (wrong side)

Leave a 5 cm opening for turning

② Cut the corners of the corners

③ Cut the margins 0.7 cm from the seam

13 cm

② Poke

0.5 cm

0.5

11 cm

① Turn on the right side

SEW THE POCKET ON THE BODY

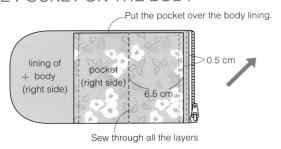

Put the pocket over the body lining.

lining of body (right side)

pocket (right side)

0.5 cm

6.5 cm

Sew through all the layers

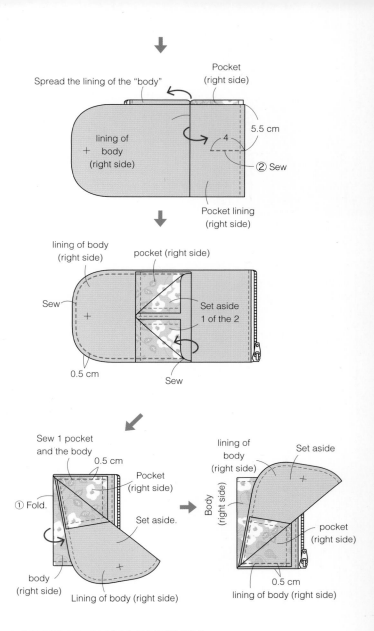

Spread the lining of the "body"

Pocket (right side)

lining of body (right side)

5.5 cm

4

② Sew

Pocket lining (right side)

lining of body (right side)

pocket (right side)

Sew

Set aside 1 of the 2

0.5 cm

Sew

Sew 1 pocket and the body

0.5 cm

① Fold.

Pocket (right side)

Set aside.

body (right side)

Lining of body (right side)

lining of body (right side)

Set aside

Body (right side)

pocket (right side)

0.5 cm

lining of body (right side)

5 FIX THE PUSH-BUTTON

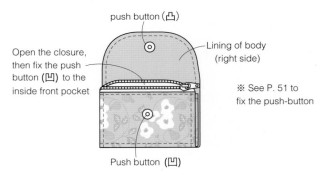

push button (凸)

Open the closure, then fix the push button (凹) to the inside front pocket

Lining of body (right side)

※ See P. 51 to fix the push-button

Push button (凹)

Completed!

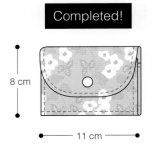

8 cm

11 cm

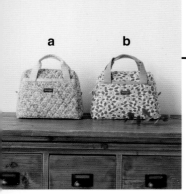

TRAPEZOIDAL BOSTON MINI BAGS

NO 6 PAGE 20

NO 6 PAGE 20

Full size patterns in side A

Body, lining of body, pocket, lining of pocket

SUPPLIES (a)

60 x 80 cm of printed quilted fabric (fabric A)
70 x 90 cm from Oxford plain blue (fabric B)
1 zipper 35 cm long 1 label 1.5 x 4.5 cm

60 x 80 cm of quilted fabric with flowers (fabric A)
70 x 90 cm of Oxford plain pink (fabric B)
1 zipper 35 cm long 1 label 1.5 x 4.5 cm

※ There are no patterns for the handle and the leg for this model. Mark them directly on the fabric.
※ The numbers in the square correspond to the seam margins. Add 1 cm margin, unless otherwise indicated.
※ The margin is included in the pocket pattern.

Cutting Plans

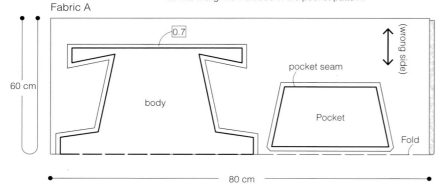

Fabric A

Fabric B

2 MAKE THE POCKETS

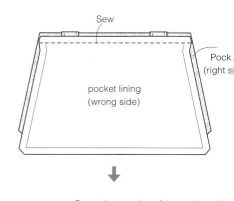

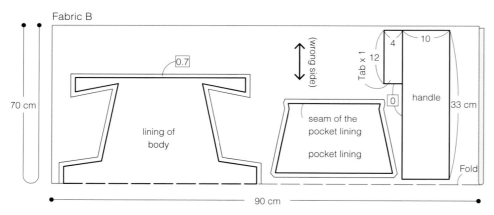

Cover the opening of the pocket with the lining, then fold the lining over the back of the pocket.

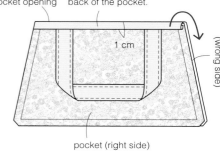

pocket opening
pocket (right side)
1 cm

CONSTRUCTION

1 MAKE THE HANDLES AND ASSEMBLE THEM TO THE POCKETS

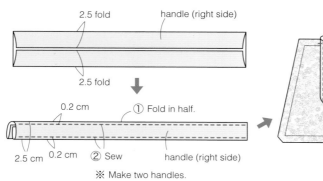

2.5 fold   handle (right side)
2.5 fold
0.2 cm   ① Fold in half.
2.5 cm   0.2 cm   ② Sew   handle (right side)
※ Make two handles.

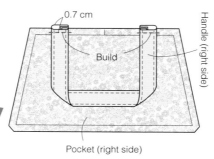

0.7 cm
Build
Handle (right side)
Pocket (right side)

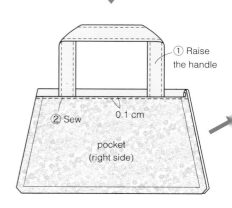

① Raise the handle
② Sew   0.1 cm
pocket (right side)

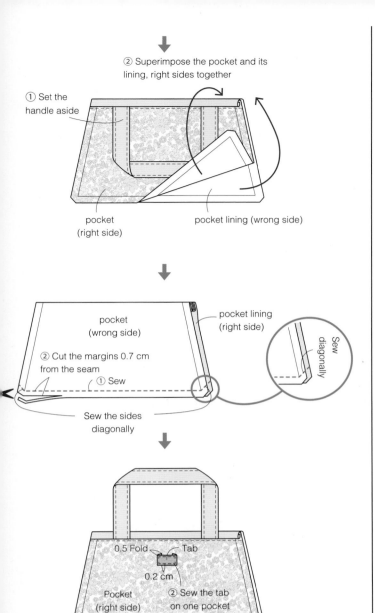

↓

② Superimpose the pocket and its
lining, right sides together

① Set the
handle aside

pocket
(right side)

pocket lining (wrong side)

↓

pocket
(wrong side)

pocket lining
(right side)

② Cut the margins 0.7 cm
from the seam

① Sew

Sew the sides
diagonally

Sew
diagonally

↓

0.5 Fold   Tab

0.2 cm

Pocket
(right side)

② Sew the tab
on one pocket

① Turn right side out

※ Make one other pocket in the same way.

SEW THE POCKETS ON THE BODY

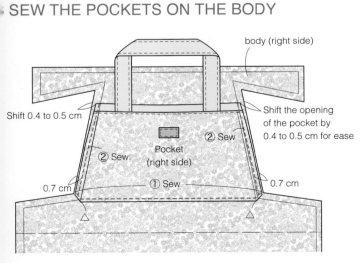

body (right side)

Shift the opening
of the pocket by
0.4 to 0.5 cm for ease

Shift 0.4 to 0.5 cm

② Sew

Pocket
(right side)

② Sew

0.7 cm

① Sew

0.7 cm

※ Sew the other pocket in the same way.

4 SEW THE ZIPPER

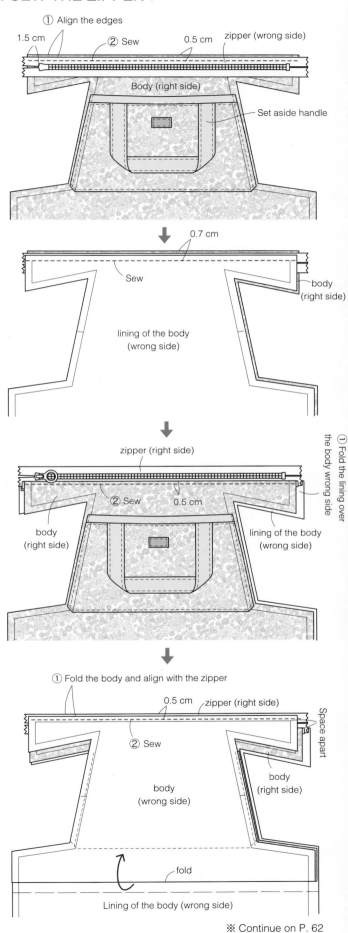

① Align the edges

1.5 cm

② Sew

0.5 cm

zipper (wrong side)

Body (right side)

Set aside handle

↓

0.7 cm

Sew

body
(right side)

lining of the body
(wrong side)

↓

zipper (right side)

② Sew

0.5 cm

body
(right side)

lining of the body
(wrong side)

① Fold the lining over
the body wrong side

↓

① Fold the body and align with the zipper

0.5 cm   zipper (right side)

② Sew

Space apart

body
(wrong side)

body
(right side)

fold

Lining of the body (wrong side)

※ Continue on P. 62

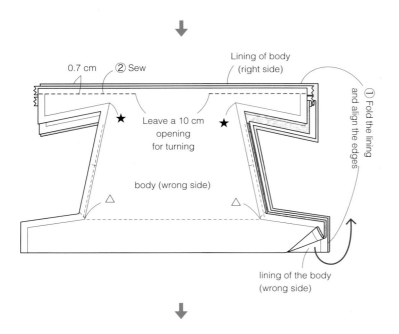

↓

0.7 cm ② Sew Lining of body (right side)

★ Leave a 10 cm opening for turning ★ ① Fold the lining and align the edges

body (wrong side)

△ △

lining of the body (wrong side)

↓

Tab 2.5 cm Fold in half
1 cm

※ See P. 69

① Turn right side out

② Sew 10 opening for turning
0.5 cm 0.5 cm

Body (right side) 1.4 cm

Lining of the body zipper (wrong side)

③ Sew on the pads at the ends of the zipper

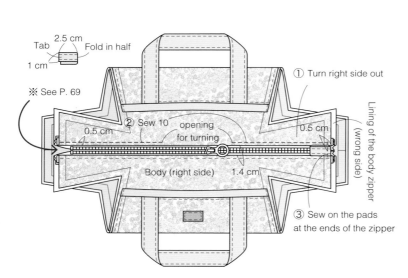

5 FOLD BACK THE BODY, THEN SEW THE ENDS OF THE ZIPPER

① Turn wrong side out. Fold over to arrange the body, right sides together. Fold the lining, right sides together.

Lining of body (right side)

Body (wrong side) Body (right side)

② Sew through all the layers.

Lining of body (bottom, wrong side)

② Sew through all the layers.

Zipper (wrong side)

△ △ △

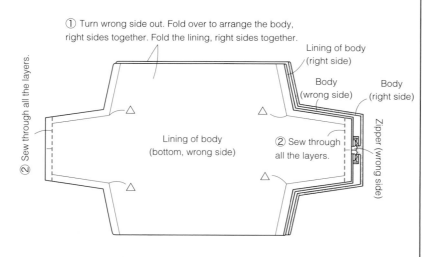

6 SEW THE BELLOWS

Fold the bellows of the body and the lining, then sew through all the layers.

Match the same symbols ★ and △.

★ ★

Align the side and the mark.

body (wrong side)

△ △

Lining of the body (wrong side)

※ Sew the other bellow in the same way.

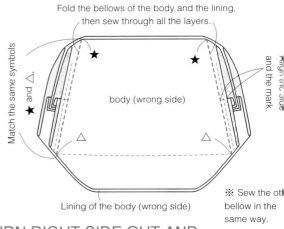

7 TURN RIGHT SIDE OUT AND CLOSE THE OPENING

Turn right side out, then close the opening (see p. 11)

lining of body (right side)

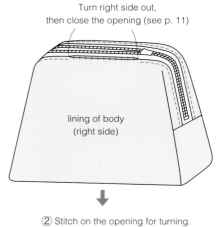

↓

② Stitch on the opening for turning.
0.5 cm

① Turn right side out.

body (right side)

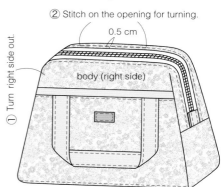

Completed!

Fold the middle of the handles in half, then stitch on 9 cm.

17 cm

25 cm 10 cm

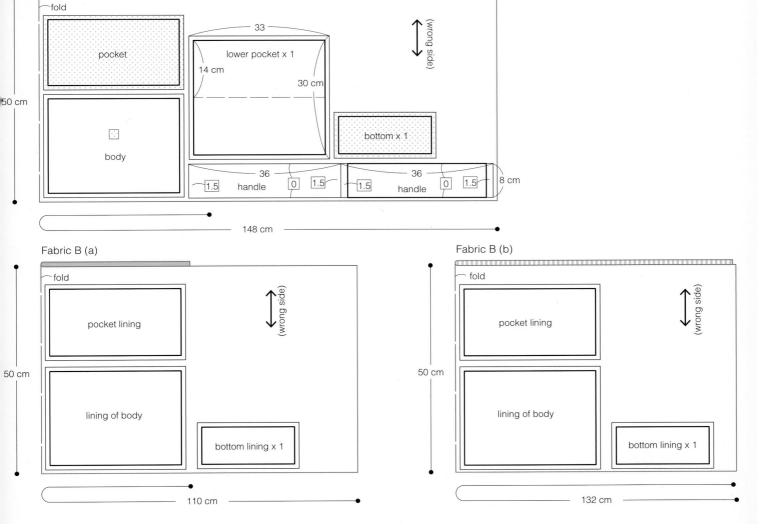

MULTIPOCKET YOKE BAGS

NO 7 PAGE 22

SUPPLIES (a)

50 x 148 cm of Oxford with flowers (fabric A)
50 x 110 cm of Oxford khaki (fabric B)
40 x 94 cm of iron-on canvas
80 cm khaki twill ribbon 2 cm wide
170 cm unbleached cord ø 0.5 cm
2 push buttons ø 1.4 cm

SUPPLIES (b)

50 x 148 cm of embroidered cotton (fabric A)
50 x 132 cm of striped linen (fabric B)
40 x 94 cm of fusible fabric
80 cm of ecru twill ribbon 2 cm wide 170 cm
of dark blue cord ø 0.5 cm 2 push button of
ø 1.4 cm

PREPARATION

Heat-seal the pocket, bottom and location of the body push button.

※ There are no patterns for the inside pocket and for the handle for this model. Trace them directly on the fabric.
※ The numbers in the square correspond to the seam margins. Add 1 cm margin, unless otherwise indicated.
※ Heat-seal the blue parts.

Cutting Plans

Fabric A

fold

pocket

lower pocket x 1
33
14 cm
30 cm
(wrong side)

body

bottom x 1

36 handle | 1.5 | 0 | 1.5
36 handle | 1.5 | 0 | 1.5
8 cm

50 cm

148 cm

Fabric B (a)

fold

pocket lining

(wrong side)

lining of body

bottom lining x 1

50 cm

110 cm

Fabric B (b)

fold

pocket lining

(wrong side)

lining of body

bottom lining x 1

50 cm

132 cm

CONSTRUCTION

1 MAKE THE HANDLES AND ASSEMBLE THEM TO THE POCKETS

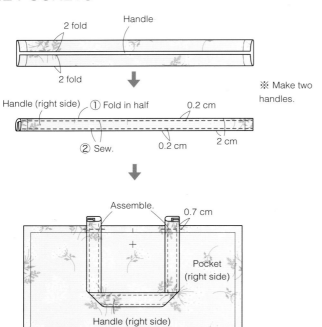

2 fold

Handle

2 fold

Handle (right side) ① Fold in half 0.2 cm

② Sew. 0.2 cm 2 cm

※ Make two handles.

Assemble. 0.7 cm

Pocket (right side)

Handle (right side)

※ Make two pieces.

2 SUPERIMPOSE THE POCKET AND ITS LINING, THEN SEW THE OPENING OF THE POCKET

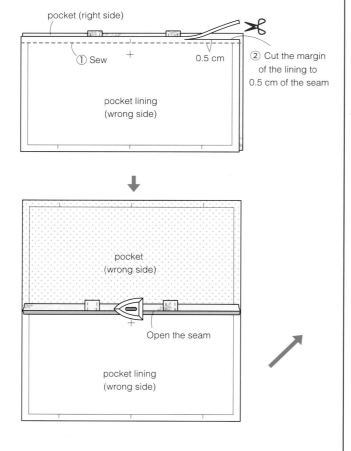

pocket (right side)

① Sew 0.5 cm

② Cut the margin of the lining to 0.5 cm of the seam

pocket lining (wrong side)

pocket (wrong side)

Open the seam

pocket lining (wrong side)

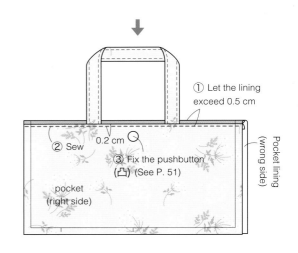

① Let the lining exceed 0.5 cm

② Sew 0.2 cm ③ Fix the pushbutton (凸) (See P. 51)

pocket (right side)

Pocket lining (wrong side)

3 ASSEMBLE THE POCKETS TO THE BODIES

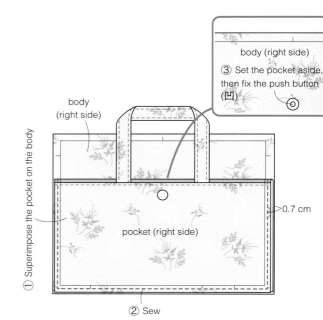

body (right side)

③ Set the pocket aside, then fix the push button (凹)

body (right side)

① Superimpose the pocket on the body

pocket (right side) 0.7 cm

② Sew

4 SEW THE INNER POCKET

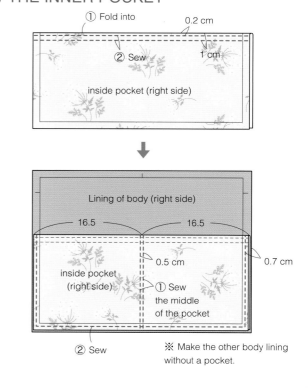

① Fold into 0.2 cm

② Sew 1 cm

inside pocket (right side)

Lining of body (right side)

16.5 16.5

0.5 cm 0.7 cm

inside pocket (right side) ① Sew the middle of the pocket

② Sew ※ Make the other body lining without a pocket.

5 SUPERIMPOSE THE BODY AND ITS LINING, THEN SEW THE OPENING OF THE BAG

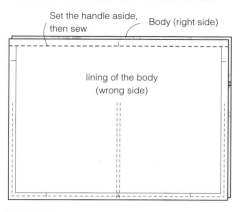

Set the handle aside, then sew

Body (right side)

lining of the body (wrong side)

6 SEW THE SIDES

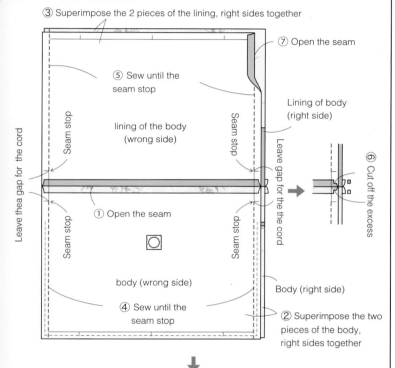

③ Superimpose the 2 pieces of the lining, right sides together

⑦ Open the seam

⑤ Sew until the seam stop

Lining of body (right side)

lining of the body (wrong side)

Seam stop

Seam stop

Leave gap for the the cord

Leave thea gap for the cord

Seam stop

Seam stop

Seam stop

⑥ Cut off the excess

① Open the seam

Body (right side)

body (wrong side)

④ Sew until the seam stop

② Superimpose the two pieces of the body, right sides together

② Topstitch the opening

Lining of body (right side)

body (right side)   0.2 cm   2 cm

① Turn right side

Set the handle aside

pocket (right side)

0.7 cm   ③ Sew

7 ASSEMBLE THE BOTTOM AND ITS LINING

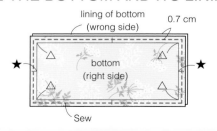

lining of bottom (wrong side)   0.7 cm

bottom (right side)

Sew

8 ASSEMBLE THE BODY AND THE BOTTOM

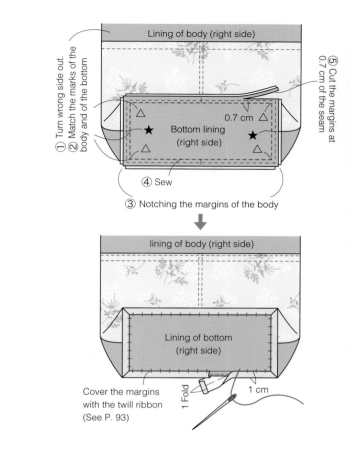

Lining of body (right side)

① Turn wrong side out.
② Match the marks of the body and of the bottom

0.7 cm

⑤ Cut the margins at 0.7 cm of the seam

Bottom lining (right side)

④ Sew

③ Notching the margins of the body

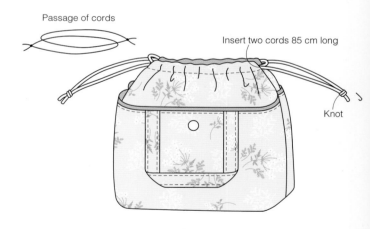

lining of body (right side)

Lining of bottom (right side)

Cover the margins with the twill ribbon (See P. 93)

1 Fold   1 cm

9 INSERT THE CORDS

Passage of cords

Insert two cords 85 cm long

Knot

Completed!

23 cm

22   9 cm

MULTIPOCKET FLAT BAG
NO 9 PAGE 32

SUPPLIES

25 x 45 cm of printed cotton (fabric A)
20 x 25 cm of striped cotton (fabric B)
20 x 25 cm of polka dot cotton (fabric C)
25 x 45 cm plain pale blue Oxford (fabric D)
1 zipper 12 cm long
1 carabiner 1.5 cm long
1 label 1.5 x 4.5 cm

※ There are no patterns for this model.
Trace all the pieces directly on the fabric.
※ The numbers in the square correspond to the seam margins.
Add 1cm margin, unless otherwise indicated.

Cutting Plans

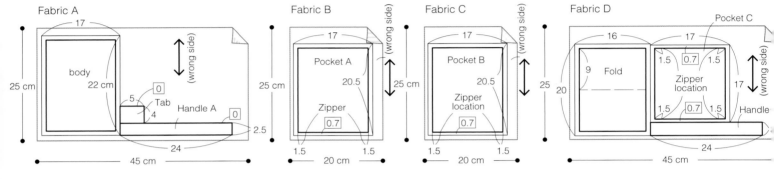

Fabric A

17
body
22 cm
(wrong side)
25 cm
5 Tab 0
4 Handle A 0
24
2.5
45 cm

Fabric B

17
Pocket A
20.5
(wrong side)
25 cm
Zipper
0.7
1.5   1.5
20 cm

Fabric C

17
Pocket B
20.5
(wrong side)
25
Zipper location
0.7
1.5   1.5
20 cm

Fabric D

16   17   Pocket C
9 Fold   1.5 0.7 1.5
20   Zipper location   17
(wrong side)
1.5 0.7 1.5
Handle
24
45 cm

CONSTRUCTION

1 MAKE THE FLAP

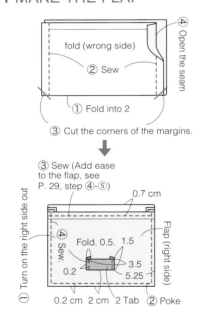

fold (wrong side)
② Sew
④ Open the seam
① Fold into 2
③ Cut the corners of the margins.

③ Sew (Add ease to the flap, see P. 29, step ④-⑤)

0.7 cm
① Turn on the right side out
④ Sew
Fold. 0.5 1.5
0.2   3.5
5.25
Flap (right side)
0.2 cm 2 cm 2 Tab ② Poke

2 MAKE THE TAB

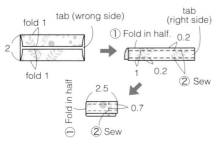

fold 1   tab (wrong side)   tab (right side)
2   ① Fold in half.   0.2
fold 1   1   0.2
② Sew
① Fold in half   2.5   0.7
② Sew

3 ASSEMBLE THE FLAP AND THE TAB TO THE BODY

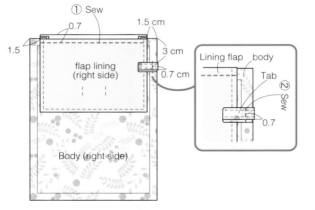

① Sew   1.5 cm
0.7
1.5   3 cm
flap lining (right side)   0.7 cm
Lining flap   body
Tab   ② Sew
0.7
Body (right side)

4 SEW THE ZIPPER TO POCKETS A, B AND C

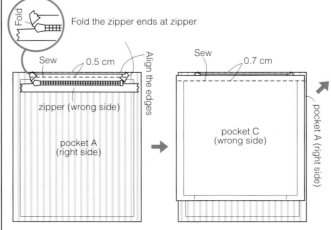

Fold   Fold the zipper ends at zipper
Sew   0.5 cm
zipper (wrong side)
pocket A (right side)
Align the edges

Sew   0.7 cm
pocket C (wrong side)
pocket A (right side)

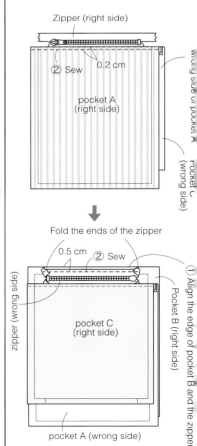

Zipper (right side)
② Sew   0.2 cm
pocket A (right side)
wrong side of pocket A
pocket C (wrong side)

Fold the ends of the zipper
0.5 cm   ② Sew
zipper (wrong side)
pocket C (right side)
pocket A (wrong side)
① Align the edge of pocket B and the zipper.
Pocket B (right side)

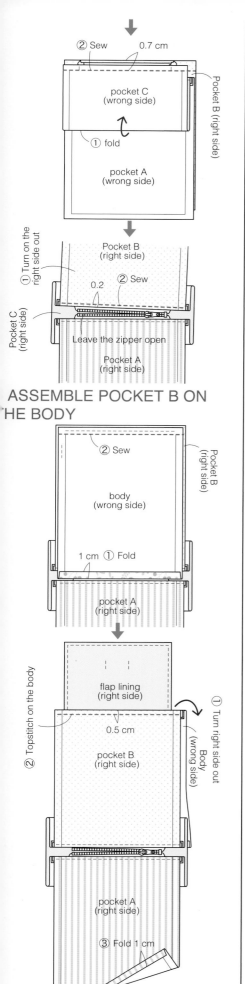

② Sew   0.7 cm

pocket C (wrong side)

① fold

pocket A (wrong side)

Pocket B (right side)

① Turn on the right side out

Pocket B (right side)

0.2   ② Sew

Pocket C (right side)

Leave the zipper open

Pocket A (right side)

ASSEMBLE POCKET B ON THE BODY

② Sew

body (wrong side)

Pocket B (right side)

1 cm ① Fold

pocket A (right side)

② Topstitch on the body

flap lining (right side)

0.5 cm

pocket B (right side)

① Turn right side out

Body (wrong side)

pocket A (right side)

③ Fold 1 cm

6 SEW THE SIDES

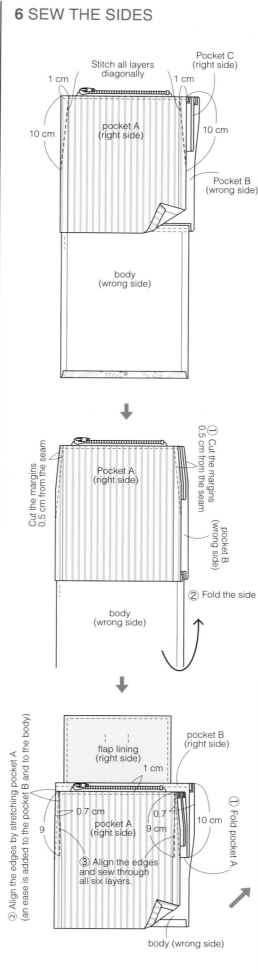

Stitch all layers diagonally

1 cm   Pocket C (right side)   1 cm

10 cm   pocket A (right side)   10 cm

Pocket B (wrong side)

body (wrong side)

Cut the margins 0.5 cm from the seam

Pocket A (right side)

① Cut the margins 0.5 cm from the seam

pocket B (wrong side)

② Fold the side

body (wrong side)

② Align the edges by stretching pocket A (an ease is added to the pocket B and to the body)

flap lining (right side)   1 cm

pocket B (right side)

0.7 cm   pocket A (right side)   0.7

9   9 cm   10 cm

③ Align the edges and sew through all six layers.

① Fold pocket A.

body (wrong side)

7 MAKE THE HANDLE section

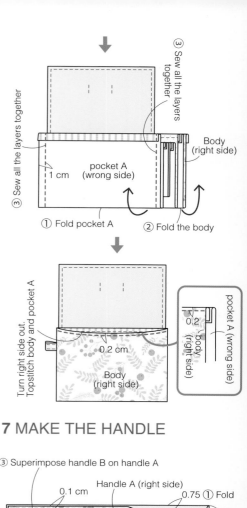

③ Sew all the layers together

pocket A (wrong side)

Body (right side)

1 cm

① Fold pocket A   ② Fold the body

Turn right side out. Topstitch body and pocket A

0.2 cm

Body (right side)

0.2 pocket A (wrong side)   body (right side)

7 MAKE THE HANDLE

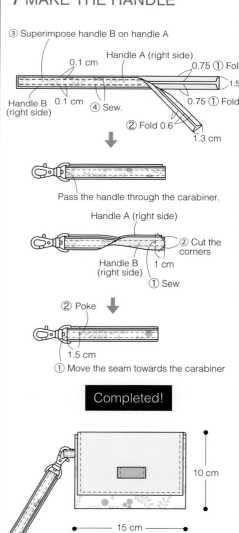

③ Superimpose handle B on handle A

0.1 cm   Handle A (right side)   0.75 ① Fold

Handle B (right side)   0.1 cm   ④ Sew.   1.5 cm

② Fold 0.6   0.75 ① Fold

1.3 cm

Pass the handle through the carabiner.

Handle A (right side)

② Cut the corners

Handle B (right side)   1 cm

① Sew

② Poke

① Move the seam towards the carabiner   1.5 cm

Completed!

10 cm

15 cm

67

(Body A, body B, lining of body)

SUPPLIES

(for 1 model, from left to right for models a / b)
15 x 50 cm of dark blue / pink printed cotton (fabric A)
20 x 30 cm Oxford solid black / red (fabric B)
30 x 40 cm of printed / striped cotton (fabric C)
20 x 80 cm of fusible fabric.
1 zipper 20 cm long 1 label 1.5 x 4.5 cm

PREPARATION

Heat-seal bodies A and B

※ There are no patterns for the tab of this model. Trace it directly on the fabric.
※ The numbers in the square correspond to the seam margins. Add 1 cm margin, unless otherwise indicated.
※ Heat-seal the blue parts.

Cutting Plans

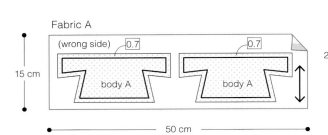

Fabric A
(wrong side) 0.7   0.7
body A   body A
15 cm
50 cm

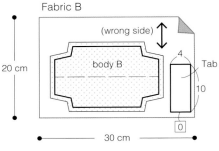

Fabric B
(wrong side)
20 cm
body B
4 Tab
10
0
30 cm

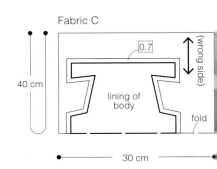

Fabric C
0.7
(wrong side)
40 cm
lining of body
fold
30 cm

CONSTRUCTION

1 ASSEMBLE BODIES A AND B

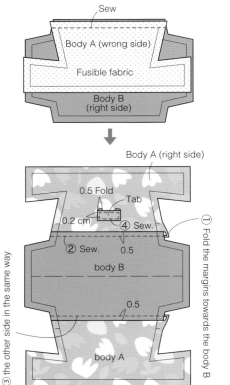

Sew
Body A (wrong side)
Fusible fabric
Body B (right side)

Body A (right side)
0.5 Fold   Tab
0.2 cm   ④ Sew.
② Sew.   0.5
body B
0.5
body A

③ the other side in the same way
① Fold the margins towards the body B

Patterns Carryover

bodies A and B   body A
★   ★   ★   ★
→
assemblage line   body B

Bodies A and B are offered in one piece. Separate the patterns on the assemblage line.

2 SEW THE ZIPPER

① Align the edges of body A and the zipper

0.5 cm   ② Poke   Zipper (wrong side)

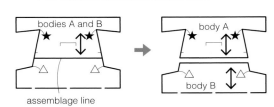

Body A (right side)

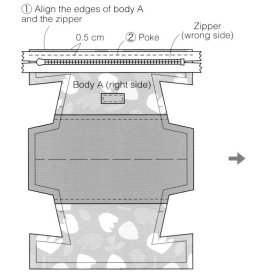

Sew   0.7 cm

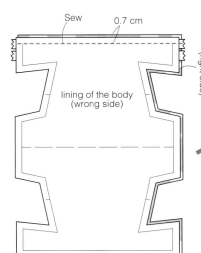

lining of the body (wrong side)

(right side)

68

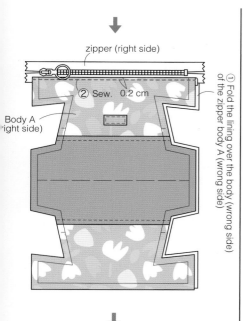

↓

zipper (right side)

② Sew. 0.2 cm

Body A (right side)

① Fold the lining over the body (wrong side) of the zipper body A (wrong side)

↓

① Fold the body and align it with the edge of the zipper

0.5 cm

Zipper (right side)

② Sew.

Body A (wrong side)

Fold

Lining of body (wrong side)

1.4 Space apart

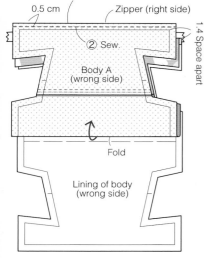

↓

② Sew

0.7 cm

lining of body (right side)

★ ★

Leave a 7 cm opening for turning.

Body A (wrong side)

△ △

lining of the body (wrong side)

Fold the body liner and align it with the edge

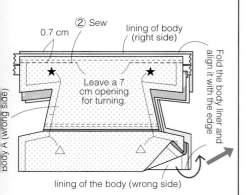

↓

② Sew

Leave the opening of 7 cm for turning. 0.2 cm

Body A (right side) 1.4 cm

① Turn right side out

Lining of the body (wrong side)

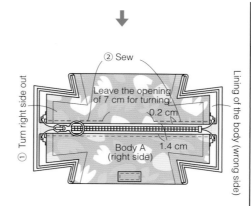

3 MAKE THE TABS

Tab (wrong side)

1 Fold

1 Fold

① Fold in half

0.2 cm

Tab (right side)

1 cm 0.2 cm

② Sew.

5 Cut Tab (right side) Fold in half

✂

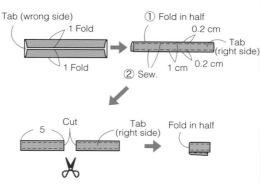

4 FOLD BACK THE BODY, THEN SEW THE ENDS OF THE ZIPPER

① Turn the body wrong side out. Fold the body, right sides together, and the lining, right sides together.

lining of body (right side)

② Insert the tab, then sew.

body B (wrong side)

0.5 cm

Tab (right side)

Leave the zipper open

Body A (right side)

↓

body A (wrong side) lining of the body (right side)

body B (wrong side) Sew through all four layers.

Poke the 4 thicknesses

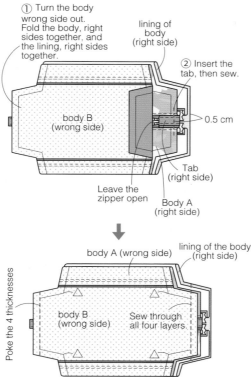

5 SEW THE BELLOWS

Fold the bellows, then sew through all four layers

lining of the body (wrong side)

★ ★

Body A (Wrong side)

△ △

Body B (wrong side)

Match the side and the marks

Align the marks ★ and △

※ Sew the other bellow in the same way

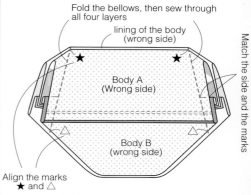

6 TURN RIGHT SIDE OUT, THEN CLOSE THE OPENING

Turn right side out, then close the opening. (See P. 11)

Lining of body (right side)

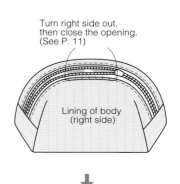

↓

② Stitch closed the opening.

0.2 cm

① Turn right side out

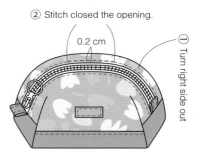

Completed!

8 cm

8 cm

14 cm

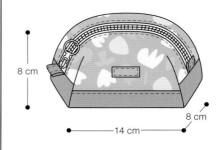

a

b

c

"SHELL" POUCHES
NO 11 PAGE 35

NO 11 PAGE 35

Full size
patterns
in side

A

(Body, body lining,
side, side lining)

SUPPLIES

(For 1 model, from left to right for a / b / c models)
20 x 54 cm of blue / light blue / white printed cotton (fabric A)
20 x 54 cm of blue / plain pink / black striped cotton (fabric B)
44 x 54 cm of plaid / floral / printed cotton (fabric C)
30 x 40 cm of fusible fabric
20 x 70 cm of fusible fleece
1 zipper of 40 cm long

PREPARATION

Heat the fleece on the bodies and sides. Heat the linings on the bodies and sides.

Cutting Plans

Fabric A

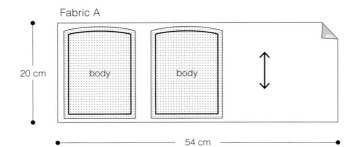

20 cm

body   body

54 cm

※ There are no patterns for the pocket and the tab for this model.
Mark them directly on the fabric.
※ The numbers in the square correspond to the seam margins. Add 1
cm margin, unless otherwise indicated.
※ Heat-seal the blue parts ☐ and the fleece on the gray parts ▦

Fabric B

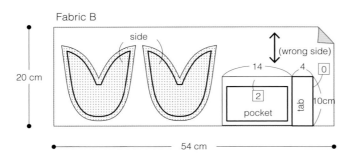

20 cm

side

(wrong side)

14   4   0

2

pocket   tab   10cm

54 cm

Fabric C

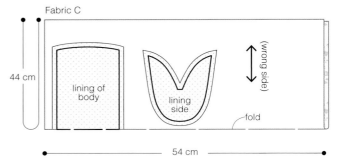

44 cm

lining of
body

lining
side

(wrong side)

fold

54 cm

CONSTRUCTION

1 SEW THE BOTTOM OF THE BODY

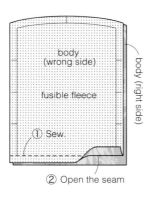

body
(wrong side)

fusible fleece

① Sew

② Open the seam

body (right side)

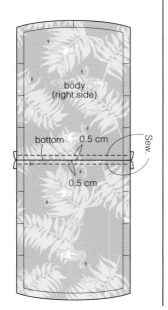

body
(right side)

bottom   0.5 cm

0.5 cm

Sew.

2 ASSEMBLE THE BODY AND THE BOTTOM

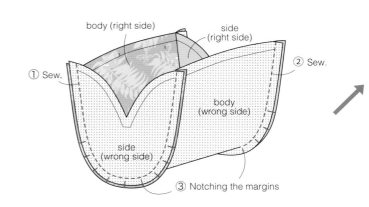

body (right side)

side
(right side)

① Sew.

② Sew.

body
(wrong side)

side
(wrong side)

③ Notching the margins

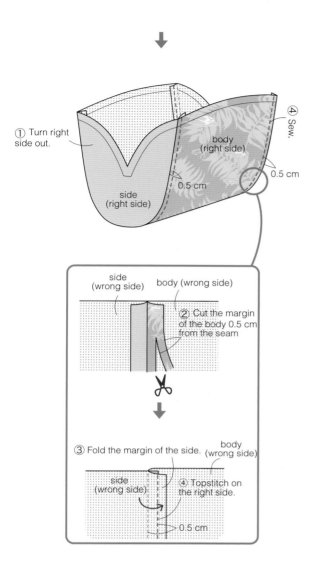

① Turn right side out.

side (right side)

body (right side)

0.5 cm

④ Sew.

0.5 cm

side (wrong side)   body (wrong side)

② Cut the margin of the body 0.5 cm from the seam

③ Fold the margin of the side.   body (wrong side)

side (wrong side)   ④ Topstitch on the right side.

0.5 cm

3 ASSEMBLE THE POCKET TO THE BODY LINING

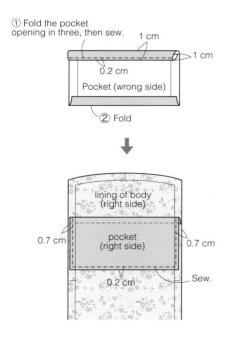

① Fold the pocket opening in three, then sew.   1 cm

1 cm

0.2 cm

Pocket (wrong side)

② Fold

lining of body (right side)

0.7 cm   pocket (right side)   0.7 cm

0.2 cm   Sew.

4 ASSEMBLE THE LININGS OF THE BODY AND SIDES

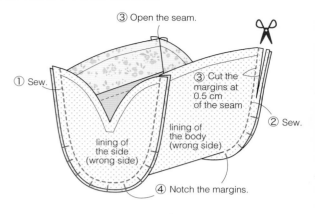

③ Open the seam.

① Sew.

③ Cut the margins at 0.5 cm of the seam

② Sew.

lining of the side (wrong side)   lining of the body (wrong side)

④ Notch the margins.

5 MAKE THE TABS

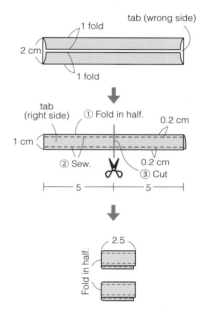

1 fold   tab (wrong side)

2 cm

1 fold

tab (right side)   ① Fold in half.   0.2 cm

1 cm

② Sew.   0.2 cm

③ Cut

5 — 5

2.5

Fold in half.

6 SEW THE TAB

7 SEW THE ZIPPER

8 ASSEMBLE THE BODY AND ITS LINING

※ See p. 72 and 73 for steps 6 to 8

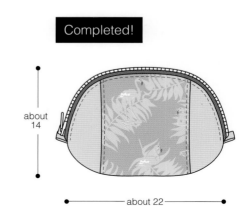

Completed!

about 14

about 22

INSTALLATION OF THE ZIPPER **NO 11 PAGE 35**

※ A different fabric and thread are used here for better visibility.

6 SEW THE TAB

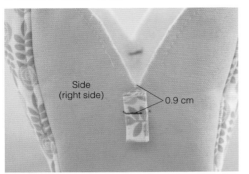

① Sew the tab onto the side.

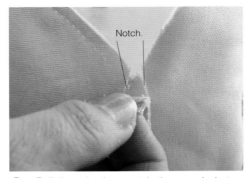

② Pull the tab, then notch the margin in two places.

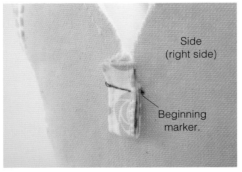

② Mark the start of the zipper on the right side.

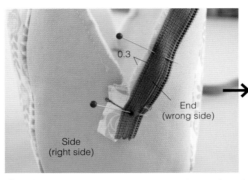

③ Superimpose the zipper on the kit opening, right sides together. Shift the zipper by 0.3 cm. Match the start marks, then pin.

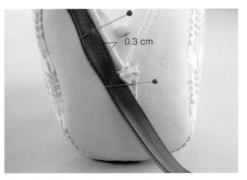

④ Continue to the other end.

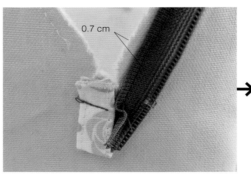

⑤ Stitch 0.7 cm from the edge.

Turn the body wrong side out.
Pin following steps ① to ④.

⑦ Sew. 0.7 cm from the edge.

7 SEW THE ZIPPER

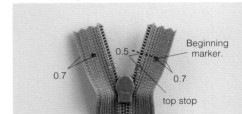

① Mark the start marker of the seam at the top end of the zipper.

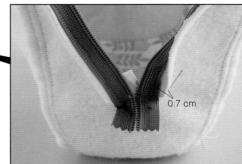

⑥

---

side (wrong side)

Sew.

⑧ Sew the side margin and the top of the zipper.

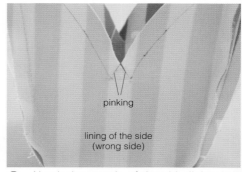

Sew.

⑨ Sew the side margin and the bottom of the zipper. Cut off the excess.

pinking

lining of the side (wrong side)

① Notch the margin of the side lining in 2 places.

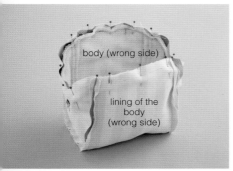

body (wrong side)

lining of the body (wrong side)

② Turn the body on the wrong side. Insert it into the lining, right sides together. Pin the opening of the kit.

Fold the triangular margin.

③ Fold the triangular margin.

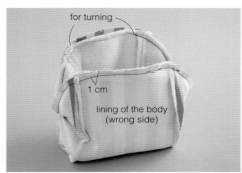

for turning

1 cm

lining of the body (wrong side)

④ Stitch the opening of the kit 1 cm from the edge, leaving a 9 cm opening for turning. Do not sew on the triangular margins.

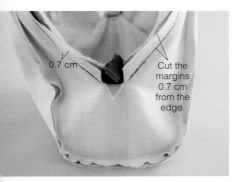

0.7 cm

Cut the margins 0.7 cm from the edge.

⑤ Cut the margins at 0.7 cm from the seam, except those of the opening to turn over.

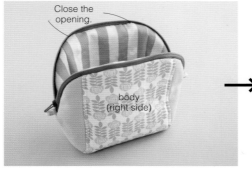

Close the opening.

body (right side)

⑥ Turn the kit right side out, then close the opening (see p 93).

ADVICE

Fleece adds thickness to the body. If it is difficult to machine sew the lining, cut the fleece close to the body seam. It is also possible to sew the lining by hand.

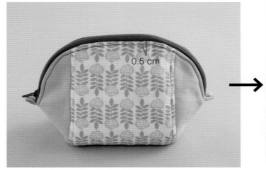

0.5 cm

⑦ Topstitch 0.5 cm from the edge.

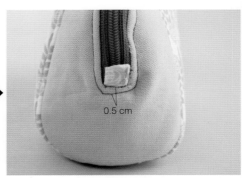

0.5 cm

BAG WITH ROUNDED OPENING
NO 12 PAGE 36

Full size patterns in side

B

(Body A, B, C, D, body
lining A, B, C, D, side A,
lining side A, side B,
lining side B)

SUPPLIES

50 x 60 cm of quilted fabric with flowers (fabric A)
50 x 60 cm of Oxford plain pink (fabric B)
20 x 50 cm of fusible fabric
2 zippers 30 cm long
1 plastic push button ø 1.3 cm
2 D-rings
1 shoulder strap 100 to 120 cm long, 1 cm wide
1 label 1.5 x 4 cm

PREPARATION

Heat-seal the linings on sides A and B, the locations of the
push button on bodies B and D.

※ There is not pattern for the pad of this model. Mark it directly on the fabric.
※ The numbers in the square correspond to the seam margins. Add 1 cm margin,
unless otherwise indicated.
※ Heat-seal the blue parts. ⬚

Cutting Plans

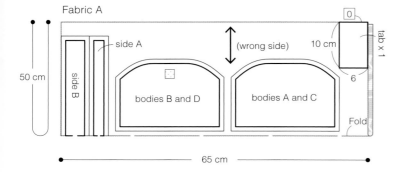

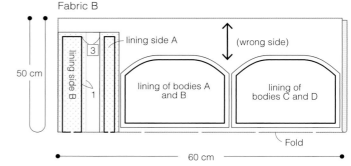

CONSTRUCTION

1 ASSEMBLE THE ZIPPER WITH BODIES A AND B TO MAKE THE BAG 1

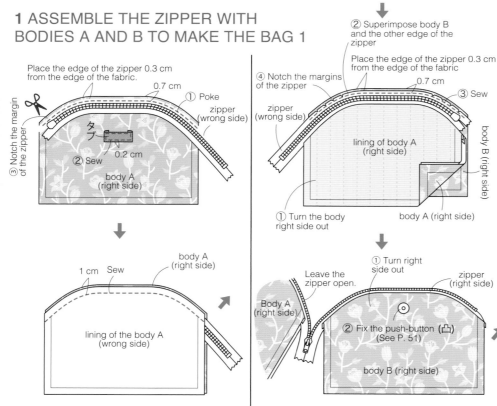

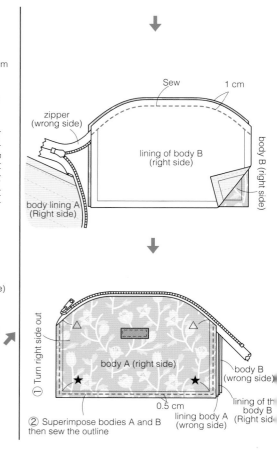

2 MAKE THE SIDE A

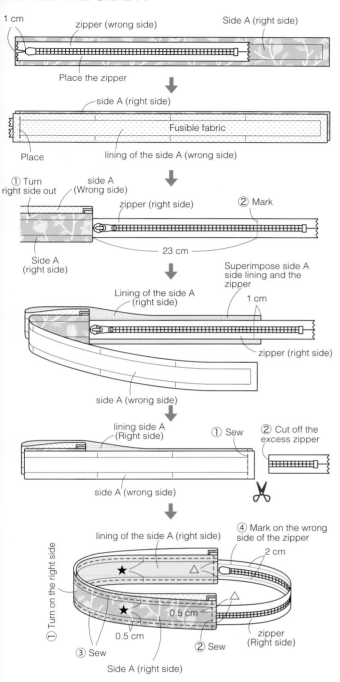

1 cm
zipper (wrong side)
Side A (right side)
Place the zipper

side A (right side)
Fusible fabric
Place
lining of the side A (wrong side)

① Turn right side out
side A (Wrong side)
zipper (right side)
② Mark
Side A (right side)
23 cm

Superimpose side A side lining and the zipper
1 cm
Lining of the side A (right side)
zipper (right side)
side A (wrong side)

lining side A (Right side)
① Sew
② Cut off the excess zipper
side A (wrong side)

lining of the side A (right side)
④ Mark on the wrong side of the zipper
2 cm
① Turn on the right side
★
△
△
★
0.5 cm
② Sew
③ Sew
0.5 cm
zipper (Right side)
Side A (right side)

3 SEW BODY C, SIDE A AND THE ZIPPER

※ See P. 76

4 SEW THE TAB TO SIDE B

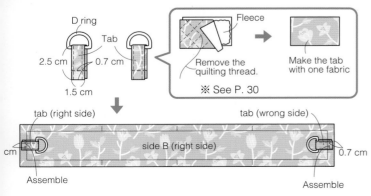

D ring
Tab
2.5 cm
0.7 cm
1.5 cm

Fleece
Remove the quilting thread.
Make the tab with one fabric
※ See P. 30

tab (right side)
tab (wrong side)
side B (right side)
cm
0.7 cm
Assemble
Assemble

5 MAKE THE SIDE B

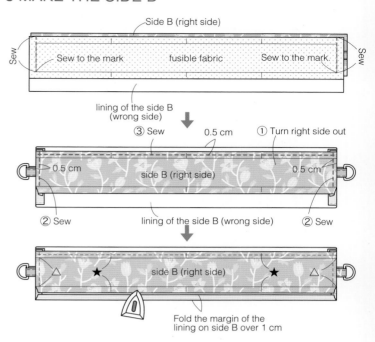

Side B (right side)
Sew
Sew to the mark
fusible fabric
Sew to the mark
Sew
lining of the side B (wrong side)

③ Sew
0.5 cm
① Turn right side out
0.5 cm
side B (right side)
0.5 cm
② Sew
lining of the side B (wrong side)
② Sew

△
★
side B (right side)
★
△
Fold the margin of the lining on side B over 1 cm

6 ASSEMBLE SIDES A AND B

7 SEW BODY D, SIDE AND ZIPPER

8 SEW SIDE B AND THE BAG 1

※ See P. 76 and 77 for steps 6 to 8

Completed!

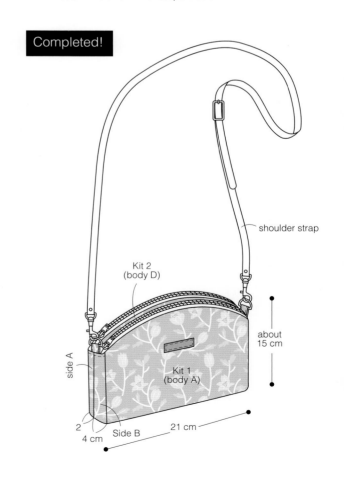

shoulder strap
Kit 2 (body D)
side A
Kit 1 (body A)
about 15 cm
2
4 cm
Side B
21 cm

SIDE SEAM `NO 12 PAGE 36`

※ A different wire is used here for better visibility.

3 ASSEMBLE BODY C, SIDE A AND THE ZIPPER

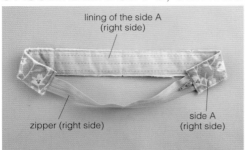

Side A (See p.75)

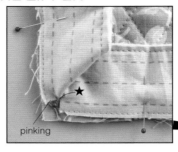

① Place the body C and the side A, right sides together. Notch the marks on the side (★), then pin. Align the mark of the zipper (see page 75) and body finish line C, then pin.

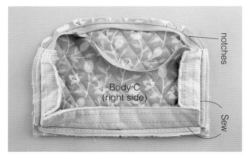

② Sew all around. Notch the zipper margin to 0.2 cm.

③ Stick adhesive tape on the side corners to avoid sewing them.

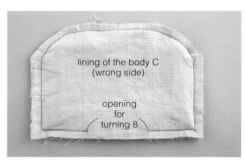

④ Assemble the piece from step ③ and the body lining C, right sides together, leaving an 8 cm opening for turning.

⑤ Remove the adhesive tape. Cut the margins to 0.7 cm of the seam. Cut the corners of the margins.

⑥ Turn right side out.

6 ASSEMBLE SIDES A AND B

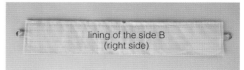

Side B (See p. 75)

7 ASSEMBLE BODY D, SIDE AND ZIPPER

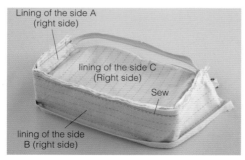

① Superimpose sides A and B, right sides together, then sew.

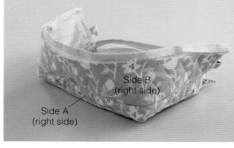

② Turn right side out.

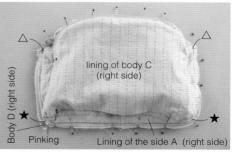

① Place Body D and the lining of side B, right sides together. Notch the marks on the side (★), then pin. Match the marks of the zipper (see page 75) and body finish line D, then pin.

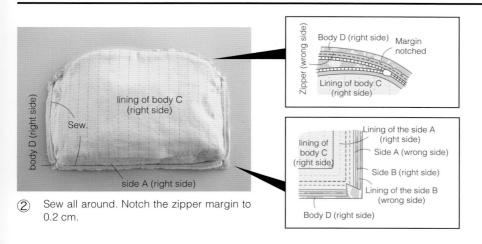

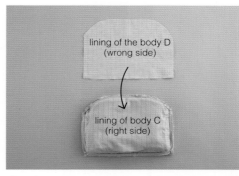

② Sew all around. Notch the zipper margin to 0.2 cm.

③ Superimpose the lining of body D and the lining of the body b, right sides together.

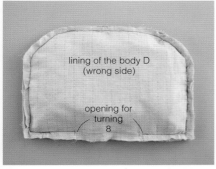

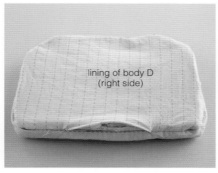

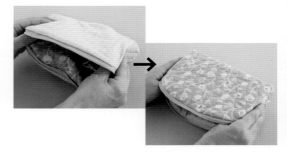

④ Sew the outline, leaving an 8 cm opening for turning.

⑤ Cut the margins at 0.7 cm of the seam. Cut the corners of the margins. Turn right side out the opening.

⑥ Turn the body right side out.

8 ASSEMBLE SIDE B AND THE BAG 1

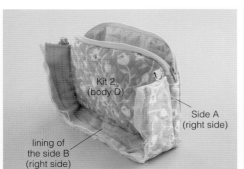

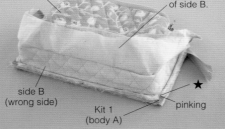

⑦ Kit 2 is finished.

① Superimpose side B and the kit 1 (body A), right sides together. Notch the marks on the side (★). Set the lining of side B aside, then sew.

② Cut off the excess from the zipper.

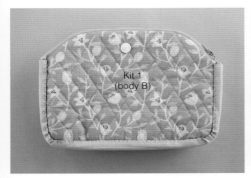

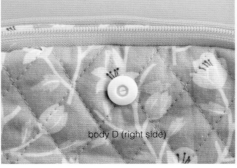

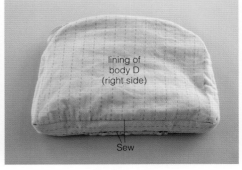

③ Cover the margins with Lining of Side B (See p. 93)

④ Insert your hand into the opening for turning and fix the push button (凹) on body D (see p. 51).

⑤ Turn kit 2 over the lining, then close the openings.

77

MULTIPOCKET TOTES
NO 13 PAGE 38

(Body, body lining, side, si... lining, bottom, facing, pock... pocket lining, side pocket... side pocket lining, strap)

SUPPLIES (a)

60 x 148 cm of dark green Oxford (fabric A)
60 x 110 cm of printed cotton (fabric B)
60 x 94 cm of fusible fabric

SUPPLIES (b)

60 x 148 cm of pink Oxford (fabric A)
60 x 110 cm of flowers cotton (fabric B)
60 x 94 cm of fusible fabric

PREPARATION

Heat-seal the body, sides and handles.

Cutting Plans

Fabric A

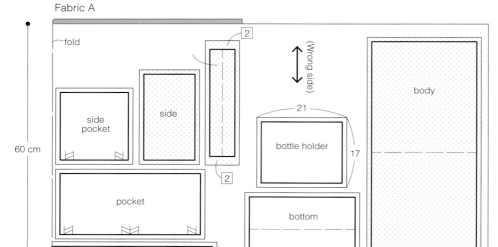

※ There is no pattern for the bottle holder of this model.
Mark it directly on the fabric.
※ The numbers in the square correspond to the seam margins.
Add 1 cm margin, unless otherwise indicated.
※ Heat-seal the blue parts. ⬚

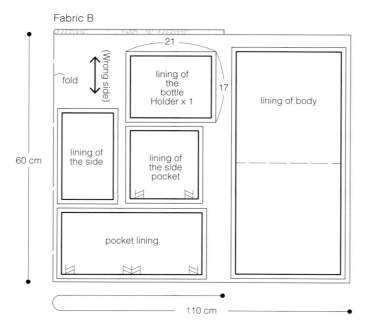

CONSTRUCTION

1 MAKE THE POCKETS

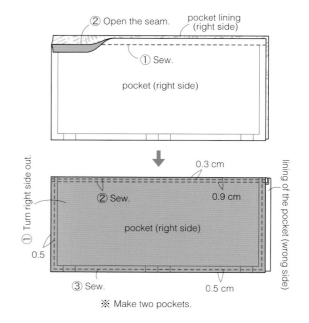

② Open the seam. pocket lining (right side)
① Sew.
pocket (right side)

① Turn right side out.
0.3 cm
② Sew. 0.9 cm
lining of the pocket (wrong side)
pocket (right side)
0.5
③ Sew. 0.5 cm

※ Make two pockets.

2 ASSEMBLE THE POCKETS TO THE BODIES

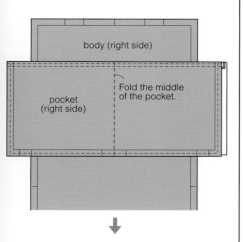

body (right side)

pocket (right side)

Fold the middle of the pocket.

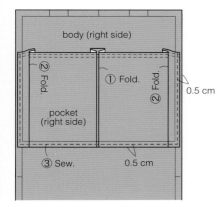

body (right side)

② Fold

① Fold.

② Fold.

0.5 cm

pocket (right side)

③ Sew.

0.5 cm

※ Sew the other pocket in the same way.

3 ASSEMBLE THE BOTTOM TO THE BODY

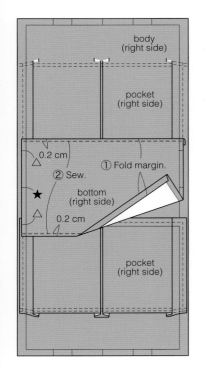

body (right side)

pocket (right side)

0.2 cm

① Fold margin.

② Sew.

★

bottom (right side)

0.2 cm

pocket (right side)

4 SEW THE HANDLES

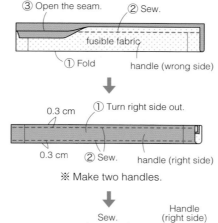

③ Open the seam.

② Sew.

fusible fabric

① Fold

handle (wrong side)

0.3 cm

① Turn right side out.

0.3 cm

② Sew.

handle (right side)

※ Make two handles.

Handle (right side)

Sew.

0.5

body (right side)

※ Sew the other handle in the same way.

5 SEW THE SIDE POCKETS

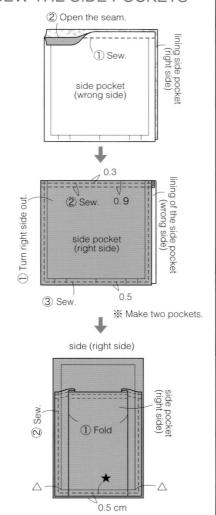

② Open the seam.

① Sew.

side pocket (wrong side)

lining side pocket (right side)

0.3

② Sew.

0.9

side pocket (right side)

lining of the side pocket (wrong side)

① Turn right side out.

③ Sew.

0.5

※ Make two pockets.

side (right side)

② Sew.

① Fold

side pocket (right side)

★

△   △

0.5 cm

6 ASSEMBLE THE BODY AND THE SIDES

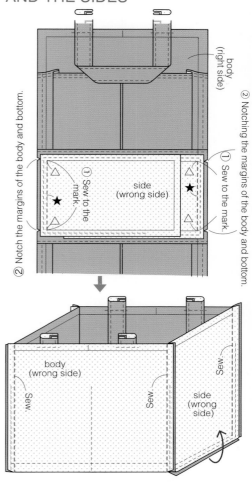

body (right side)

② Notching the margins of the body and bottom.

① Sew to the mark.

② Notch the margins of the body and bottom.

① Sew to the mark.

★

side (wrong side)

★

body (wrong side)

Sew.

Sew.

side (wrong side)

Sew.

7 MAKE THE BOTTLE HOLDER

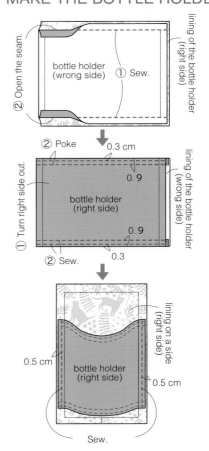

② Open the seam.

bottle holder (wrong side)

① Sew.

lining of the bottle holder (right side)

② Poke

0.3 cm

0.9

bottle holder (right side)

lining of the bottle holder (wrong side)

① Turn right side out.

② Sew.

0.3

0.9

lining on a side (right side)

0.5 cm

bottle holder (right side)

0.5 cm

Sew.

8 MAKE THE LINING

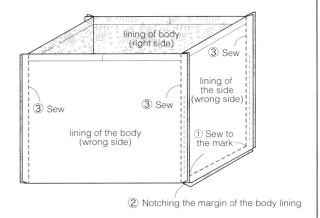

lining of body (right side)

③ Sew

lining of the side (wrong side)

③ Sew

③ Sew

lining of the body (wrong side)

① Sew to the mark

② Notching the margin of the body lining

9 SEW THE MARGINS OF THE BAG AND OF THE LINING

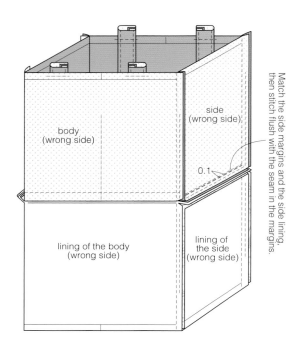

body (wrong side)

side (wrong side)

0.1

lining of the body (wrong side)

lining of the side (wrong side)

Match the side margins and the side lining, then stitch flush with the seam in the margins.

10 MAKE THE FACING

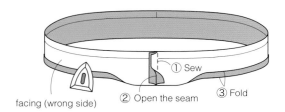

facing (wrong side)

① Sew

② Open the seam

③ Fold

11 SEW THE FACING AT THE OPENING OF THE BAG

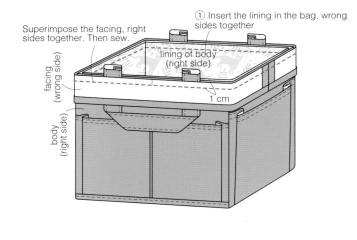

Superimpose the facing, right sides together. Then sew.

① Insert the lining in the bag, wrong sides together

facing (wrong side)

lining of body (right side)

body (right side)

1 cm

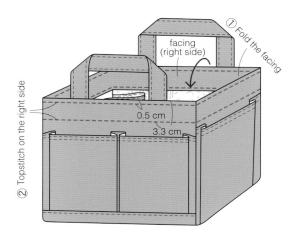

② Topstitch on the right side

facing (right side)

① Fold the facing

0.5 cm

3.3 cm

Completed!

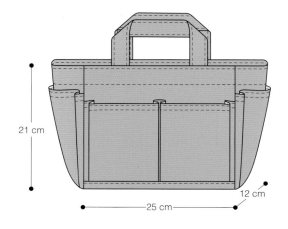

21 cm

25 cm

12 cm

SUPPLIES

20 x 109 cm of cotton with flowers (fabric A)
20 x 100 cm of striped cotton (fabric B)
20 x 70 cm of pink Oxford (fabric C)
15 x 30 cm of light blue cotton (fabric D)
30 x 108 cm of fusible fabric
120 cm of unbleached cord ø 0.5 cm

PREPARATION

Heat-seal the body, bottom and bottom lining.

※ There are no patterns for pockets A and B, the pouch, the slide and the handle for this model. Mark them directly on the fabric.
※ The numbers in the square correspond to the seam margins.
Add 1 cm margin, unless otherwise indicated.
※ The margin is included in bottom pattern.
※ Heat-seal the blue parts. ⬚

Cutting Plans

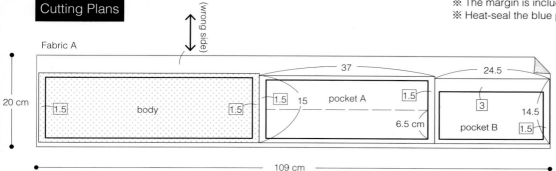

Fabric A

20 cm

1.5 body 1.5

1.5 15 37 pocket A 1.5
6.5 cm

24.5
3 14.5
pocket B 1.5

109 cm

(wrong side)

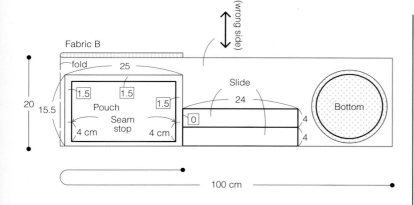

Fabric B

(wrong side)

20 15.5

fold 25
1.5 1.5
Pouch 1.5
Seam stop
4 cm 4 cm

Slide
24
0
4
4

Bottom

100 cm

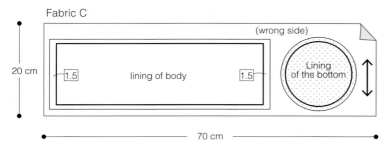

Fabric C

(wrong side)

20 cm

1.5 lining of body 1.5

Lining of the bottom

70 cm

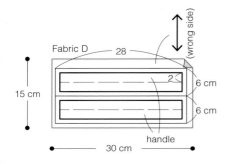

Fabric D

28
2
6 cm
6 cm
handle

15 cm

30 cm

(wrong side)

CONSTRUCTION

1 MAKE THE POCKET

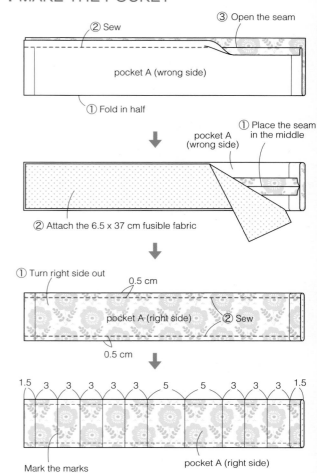

② Sew ③ Open the seam

pocket A (wrong side)

① Fold in half

pocket A (wrong side) ① Place the seam in the middle

② Attach the 6.5 x 37 cm fusible fabric

① Turn right side out 0.5 cm

pocket A (right side) ② Sew

0.5 cm

1.5 3 3 3 3 3 5 5 3 3 3 1.5

Mark the marks pocket A (right side)

2 ASSEMBLE THE POCKET TO THE BODY LINING

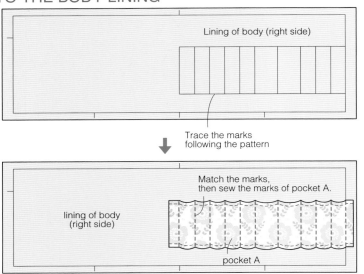

Lining of body (right side)

Trace the marks following the pattern

Match the marks, then sew the marks of pocket A.

lining of body (right side)

pocket A

3 ASSEMBLE THE POCKET B ON THE LINING

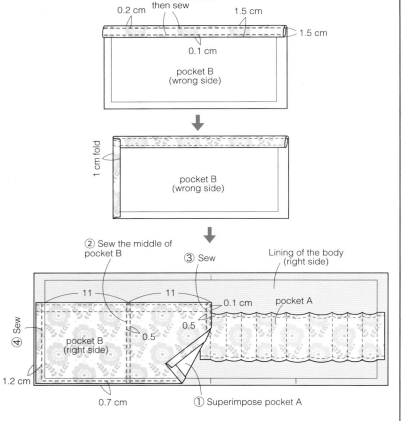

Fold over twice then sew

0.2 cm   1.5 cm

1.5 cm

0.1 cm

pocket B (wrong side)

1 cm fold

pocket B (wrong side)

② Sew the middle of pocket B

③ Sew

Lining of the body (right side)

11   11

0.1 cm

pocket A

④ Sew

0.5

0.5

pocket B (right side)

1.2 cm

0.7 cm

① Superimpose pocket A

4 SEW THE SIDES OF THE LINING

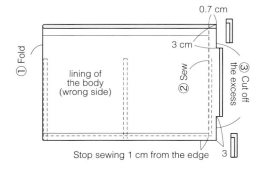

0.7 cm

3 cm

① Fold

lining of the body (wrong side)

② Sew

③ Cut off the excess

Stop sewing 1 cm from the edge

3

5 SEW THE HANDLES

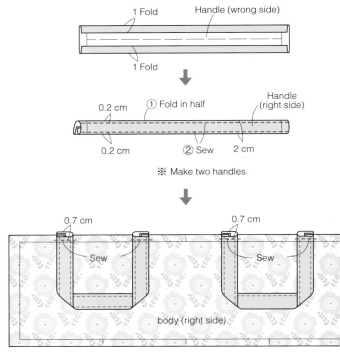

1 Fold   Handle (wrong side)

1 Fold

0.2 cm   ① Fold in half   Handle (right side)

0.2 cm

② Sew   2 cm

※ Make two handles.

0.7 cm   0.7 cm

Sew   Sew

body (right side)

6 SEW THE SIDE OF THE BODY

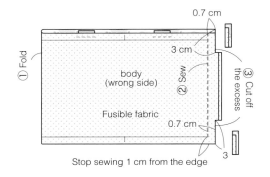

0.7 cm

3 cm

① Fold

body (wrong side)

② Sew

③ Cut off the excess

Fusible fabric

0.7 cm

Stop sewing 1 cm from the edge

3

7 ASSEMBLE THE BODY AND THE BOTTOM

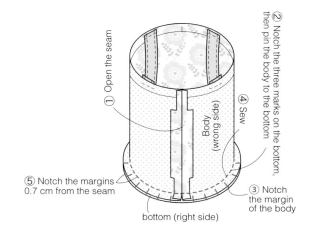

① Open the seam

② Notch the three marks on the bottom, then pin the body to the bottom.

Body (wrong side)

④ Sew

⑤ Notch the margins 0.7 cm from the seam

③ Notch the margin of the body

bottom (right side)

※ Assemble the body and bottom liners in the same way.

SUPERIMPOSE THE BODY AND TS LINING, WRONG SIDES TOGETHER, THEN SEW THE OPENING OF THE BAG

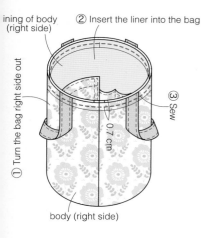

lining of body (right side)
② Insert the liner into the bag
① Turn the bag right side out
③ Sew
0.7 cm
body (right side)

MAKE THE YOKE

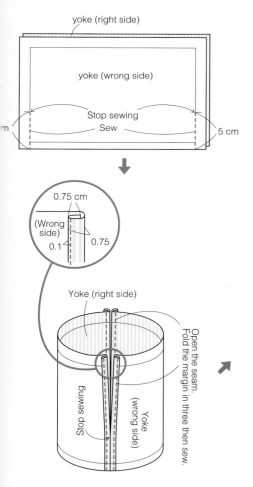

yoke (right side)
yoke (wrong side)
Stop sewing
Sew
5 cm

0.75 cm
(Wrong side)
0.1
0.75

Yoke (right side)
Stop sewing
Yoke (wrong side)
Open the seam. Fold the margin in three then sew.

0.75 cm
0.75
(Wrong side)
0.1

Fold over twice then sew

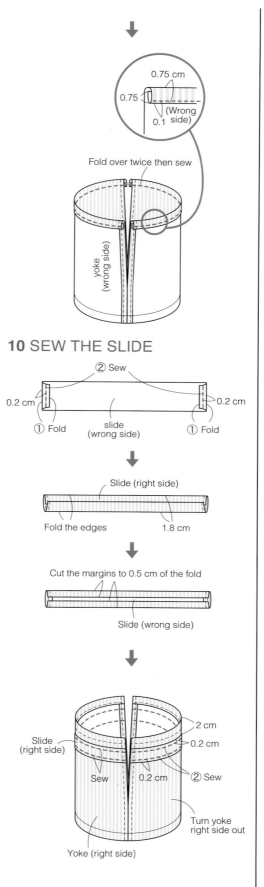

yoke (wrong side)

10 SEW THE SLIDE

② Sew
0.2 cm
① Fold
slide (wrong side)
① Fold
0.2 cm

Slide (right side)
Fold the edges
1.8 cm

Cut the margins to 0.5 cm of the fold
Slide (wrong side)

Slide (right side)
2 cm
0.2 cm
Sew
0.2 cm
② Sew
Turn yoke right side out
Yoke (right side)

11 SEW THE YOKE TO THE BAG

lining of body (right side)

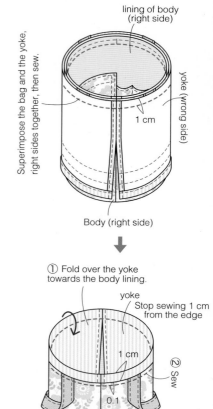

Superimpose the bag and the yoke, right sides together, then sew.
yoke (wrong side)
1 cm
Body (right side)

① Fold over the yoke towards the body lining.
yoke
Stop sewing 1 cm from the edge
1 cm
② Sew
0.1
Body (right side)

12 INSERT THE CORDS

Completed

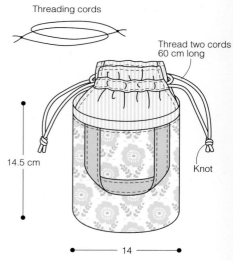

Threading cords
Thread two cords 60 cm long
14.5 cm
Knot
14

83

STORAGE BOX
NO 15A PAGE 42

Full size
patterns
in side

Body, body lining, side,
bottom lining

SUPPLIES
20 x 60 cm of yellow Oxford (fabric A)
30 x 90 cm of striped cotton (fabric B)
15 x 110 cm of flower cotton (fabric C)
30 x 94 cm of fusible fabric
1 leather handle with carabiners

PREPARATION
Heat the body and the bottom (without margin)

Cutting Plans

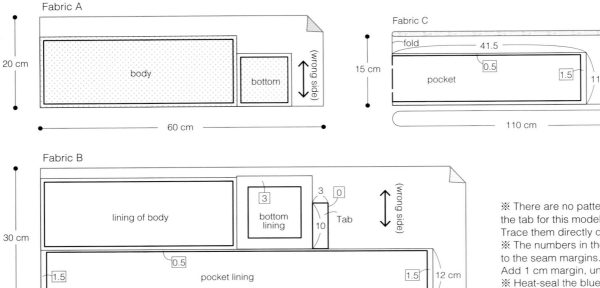

Fabric A
20 cm | 60 cm
body | bottom | (wrong side)

Fabric C
15 cm | fold | 41.5 | 0.5 | pocket | 1.5 | 11 | (wrong side) | 110 cm

Fabric B
30 cm | lining of body | 3 | bottom lining | 3 | 0 | 10 | Tab | (wrong side)
0.5 | 1.5 | pocket lining | 1.5 | 12 cm
83 | 90 cm

※ There are no patterns for the pocket and the tab for this model.
Trace them directly on the fabric.
※ The numbers in the square correspond to the seam margins.
Add 1 cm margin, unless otherwise indicated.
※ Heat-seal the blue parts. ⬚

CONSTRUCTION

1 MAKE THE POCKET

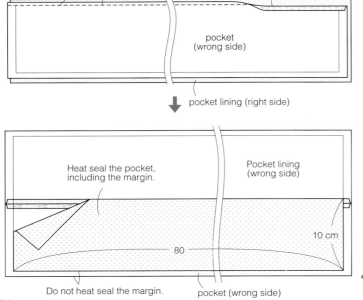

0.5 | ① Sew. | ② Open the seam
pocket (wrong side)
pocket lining (right side)

Heat seal the pocket, including the margin. | Pocket lining (wrong side)
80 | 10 cm
Do not heat seal the margin. | pocket (wrong side)

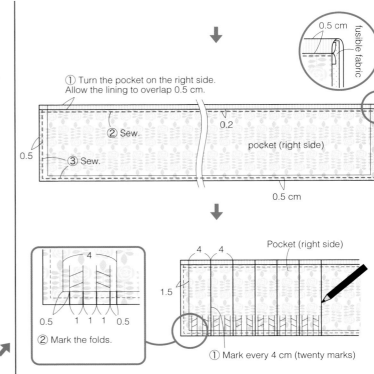

0.5 cm | fusible fabric
① Turn the pocket on the right side. Allow the lining to overlap 0.5 cm.
② Sew. | 0.2
0.5 | ③ Sew. | pocket (right side)
0.5 cm

4 | pocket (right side)
0.5 1 1 1 0.5 | 4 4
② Mark the folds. | 1.5
① Mark every 4 cm (twenty marks)

84

MAKE THE TABS

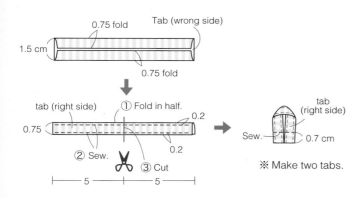

0.75 fold　　Tab (wrong side)
1.5 cm
0.75 fold

tab (right side)
0.75
① Fold in half.
② Sew.
③ Cut
0.2
0.2
5　　5

tab (right side)
Sew.
0.7 cm

※ Make two tabs.

MAKE MARKS ON THE BODY
ASSEMBLE THE POCKET AND THE TABS

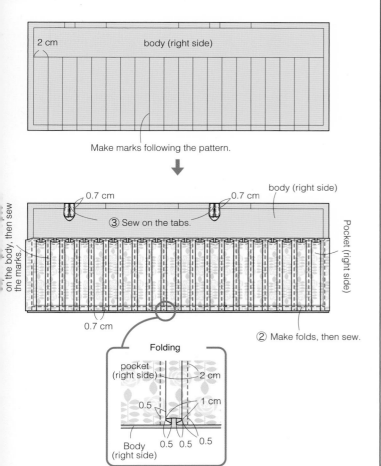

2 cm　　body (right side)

Make marks following the pattern.

on the body, then sew the marks.

0.7 cm　　0.7 cm　　body (right side)
③ Sew on the tabs.
Pocket (right side)
0.7 cm
② Make folds, then sew.

Folding
pocket (right side)　　2 cm
0.5　　1 cm
Body (right side)
0.5　0.5　0.5

SUPERIMPOSE THE BODY AND THE LINING,
RIGHT SIDES TOGETHER, THEN SEW THE OPENING

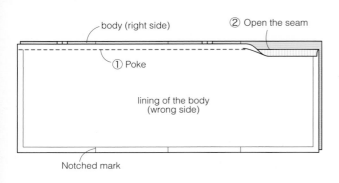

body (right side)　　② Open the seam
① Poke
lining of the body (wrong side)
Notched mark

5 SEW THE SIDE

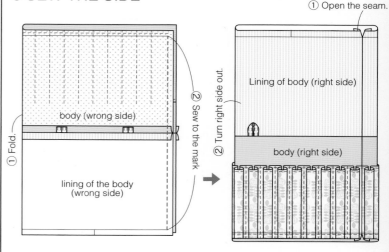

① Open the seam.
① Fold.
body (wrong side)
② Sew to the mark
lining of the body (wrong side)

② Turn right side out.
Lining of body (right side)
body (right side)

6 INSERT THE LINING INTO THE BODY, THEN TOPSTITCH THE OPENING

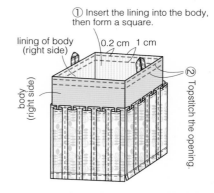

① Insert the lining into the body, then form a square.
lining of body (right side)　　0.2 cm　1 cm
body (right side)
② Topstitch the opening.

7 SEW THE CORNERS OF THE OPENING

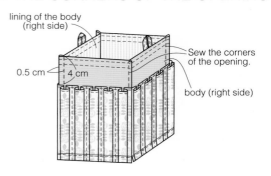

lining of the body (right side)
0.5 cm　4 cm
Sew the corners of the opening.
body (right side)

8 ASSEMBLE THE BODY AND THE BOTTOM

※ See P. 87

Completed!

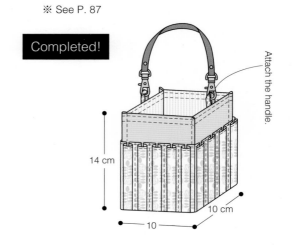

Attach the handle.
14 cm
10 cm
10

STORAGE BOX
NO 15B

SUPPLIES

30 x 100 cm of red cotton (fabric A)
15 x 80 cm of printed cotton (fabric B)
30 x 108 cm of thick fusible fabric
40 cm of red twill ribbon of 2 cm wide
1 leather strap with carabiners

PREPARATION

Heat the body and the bottom (without margin).

※ There are no patterns for the pocket and the tab for this model. Mark them directly on the fabric.
※ The numbers in the square correspond to the seam margins. Add 1 cm margin, unless otherwise indicated.
※ The margin is included in bottom pattern.
※ Heat-seal the blue parts. ▭

Cutting Plans

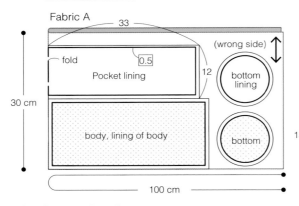

Fabric A
33
(wrong side)
fold
0.5
Pocket lining
12
bottom lining
30 cm
body, lining of body
bottom
100 cm

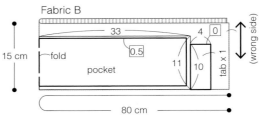

Fabric B
33
4 0
fold
0.5
pocket
11
10
tab x 1
(wrong side)
15 cm
80 cm

CONSTRUCTION

1 MAKE THE POCKET

※ See P. 84

※ Fix 10 x 64 cm of fusible fabric.

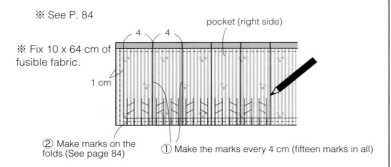

pocket (right side)
4 4
1 cm

② Make marks on the folds (See page 84)

① Make the marks every 4 cm (fifteen marks in all)

2 TO 4 See P. 85

※ Make the tabs 1 cm wide.

5 SEW THE MIDDLE BACK

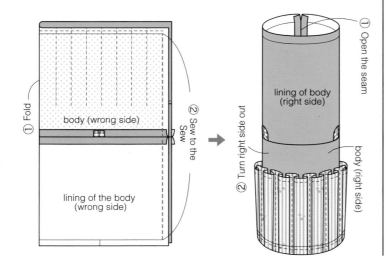

① Fold
body (wrong side)
② Sew to the Sew
lining of the body (wrong side)

① Open the seam
lining of body (right side)
body (right side)
② Turn right side out

6 INSERT THE LINING INTO THE BODY, THEN SEW THE OPENING

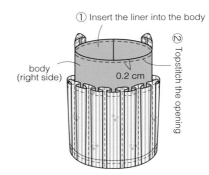

① Insert the liner into the body
② Topstitch the opening
body (right side)
0.2 cm

7 ASSEMBLE THE BODY AND THE BOTTOM

※ See P. 87

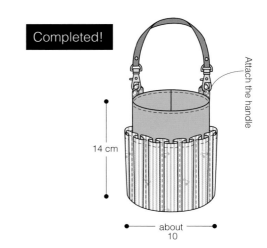

Completed!

Attach the handle
14 cm
about 10

SQUARE BOTTOM ASSEMBLY `NO 15A PAGE 42`

※ The pocket is not sewn for better visibility.

7 ASSEMBLE THE BODY AND THE BOTTOM

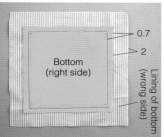

① Superimpose the bottom onto its lining, wrong sides together. Stitch on the finishing line.

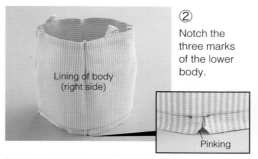

② Notch the three marks of the lower body.

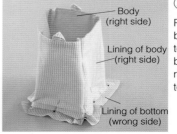

③ Pin the body to the bottom, right sides together.

④ Build 0.7 cm from the bottom edge.

⑤ Fold the edges of the bottom lining in three to cover the margins. Pin.

⑥ Sew 0.2 cm from the edge.

ROUND BOTTOM ASSEMBLY `NO 15B PAGE 42`

※ The pocket is not sewn for better visibility.

7 ASSEMBLE THE BODY AND THE BOTTOM

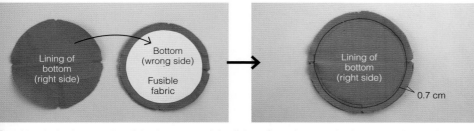

① Notch the four marks of the bottom and the lining. Superimpose the bottom and its lining, wrong sides together, then sew 0.7 cm from the edge of the bottom.

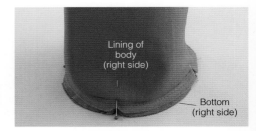

② Notch the three marks of the lower body. Pin the body and the bottom, right sides together.

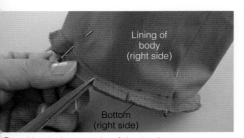

③ Notch the margin of the body.

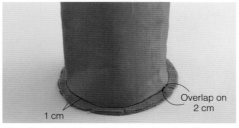

④ Sew 1 cm from the edge. Overlap the seam at the start and end by 2 cm.

⑤ Cut the bottom pattern from thick paper. Fold the twill ribbon in two. Insert the pattern into the fold, then iron to mark the curve.

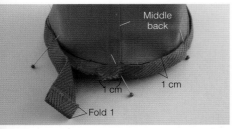

⑥ Cover the margins with the twill ribbon, then pin. Fold the end of the ribbon over 1 cm, then overlap the ends by 1 cm.

⑦ Sew the edge of the twill ribbon (see p. 93).

⑧ Sew the other edge of the twill ribbon in the same way.

WALLET WITH A TAB

NO 16 PAGE 44

SUPPLIES

40 x 110 cm of embroidered cotton (fabric A)
30 x 50 cm of flower cotton (fabric B)
30 x 50 cm of fusible fleece
1 magnetic button to sew ø 1.8 cm
1 pair of metal reinforcements 5 x 15 cm

PREPARATION

Heat seal the fleece on the tab.

Cutting Plans

※ The fabric with embroidered flowers on the borders is used for this model. Arrange the patterns according to the designs of the fabric.

※ There is no pattern for this model.
Trace all the pieces directly on the fabric.
※ The numbers in the square correspond to the seam margins.
Add 1 cm margin, unless otherwise indicated.
※ Heat seal the fleece on the blue part. ▦

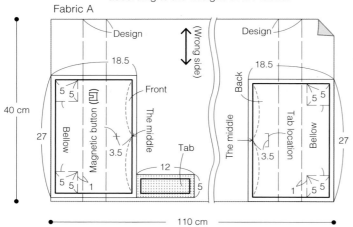

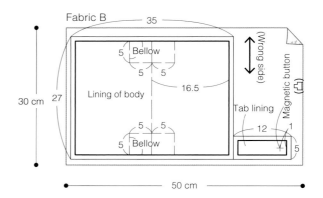

CONSTRUCTION

1 SEW THE BOTTOM OF THE BODY, THEN FIX THE FUSIBLE FLEECE

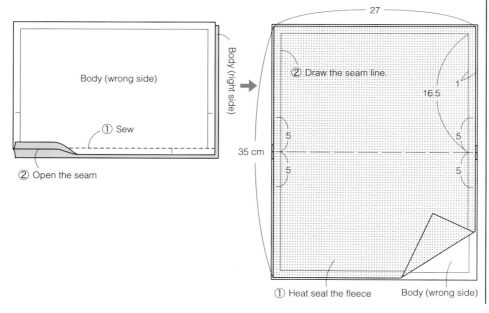

2 SUPERIMPOSE THE BODY AND THE LINING, RIGHT SIDES TOGETHER, THEN SEW THE OPENINGS

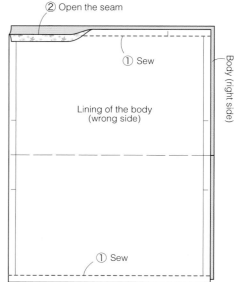

3 SEW THE SIDES

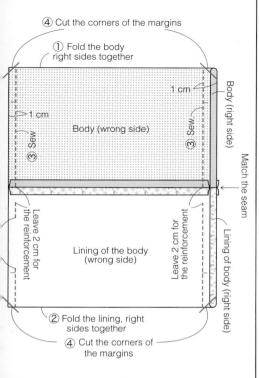

④ Cut the corners of the margins

① Fold the body right sides together

1 cm

1 cm

Body (wrong side)

③ Sew

③ Sew

Body (right side)

Match the seam

Leave 2 cm for the reinforcement

Lining of the body (wrong side)

Leave 2 cm for the reinforcement

Lining of body (right side)

② Fold the lining, right sides together

④ Cut the corners of the margins

4 SEW THE BELLOWS

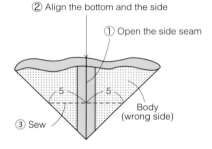

② Align the bottom and the side

① Open the side seam

5   5

③ Sew

Body (wrong side)

※ Sew the other pocket in the same way.

5 ASSEMBLE THE MARGINS OF THE BODY AND OF THE LINING

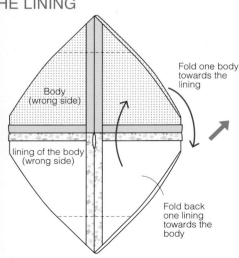

Body (wrong side)

lining of the body (wrong side)

Fold one body towards the lining

Fold back one lining towards the body

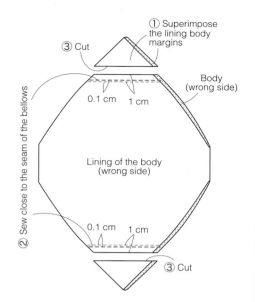

① Superimpose the lining body margins

③ Cut

0.1 cm   1 cm

Body (wrong side)

Lining of the body (wrong side)

② Sew close to the seam of the bellows

0.1 cm   1 cm

③ Cut

6 TURN RIGHT SIDE, THEN CLOSE THE OPENING

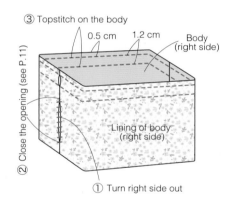

③ Topstitch on the body

0.5 cm   1.2 cm

Body (right side)

② Close the opening (see P. 11)

Lining of body (right side)

① Turn right side out

7 MAKE THE TAB

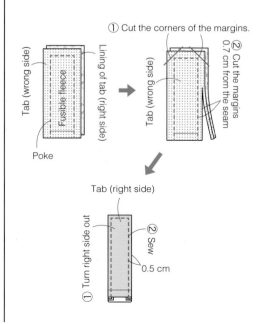

① Cut the corners of the margins.

Tab (wrong side)

Fusible fleece

Lining of tab (right side)

Poke

Tab (wrong side)

② Cut the margins 0.7 cm from the seam

Tab (right side)

① Turn right side out

② Sew

0.5 cm

---

8 SEW THE TAB IN THE BACK

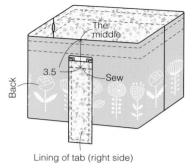

The middle

3.5

Sew

Back

Lining of tab (right side)

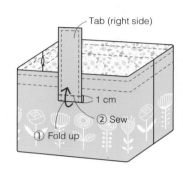

Tab (right side)

1 cm

② Sew

① Fold up

9 INSERT THE METAL REINFORCEMENTS

※ See P. 50

10 SEW THE MAGNETIC BUTTON

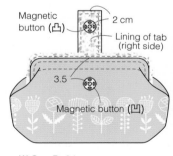

Magnetic button (凸)

2 cm

Lining of tab (right side)

3.5

Magnetic button (凹)

※ See P. 31

Completed!

11.5 cm

15

10 cm

MINI BAG
NO 17 PAGE 44

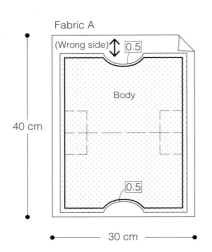

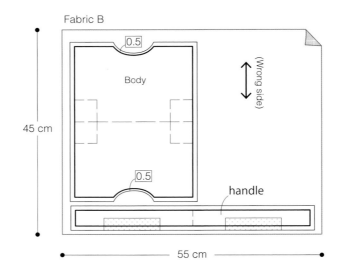

Full size patterns in side B

(Body, lining of body, handle)

SUPPLIES

30 x 40 cm of printed linen (fabric A)
45 x 55 cm of checked linen (fabric B)
40 x 50 cm of fusible interlining
1 pair of metal reinforcements 5 x 15 cm

PREPARATION

Heat seal the body and the handle.

※ The numbers in the square correspond to the seam margins.
Add 1 cm margin, unless otherwise indicated.
※ The margin is included in the handle pattern.
※ Heat-seal the blue parts. ☐

Cutting Plans

Fabric A

(Wrong side) 0.5

Body

0.5

40 cm

30 cm

Fabric B

0.5

Body

(Wrong side)

45 cm

0.5

handle

55 cm

CONSTRUCTION

1 SEW THE CURVE OF THE OPENINGS

② Notch the margins   ③ Open the seam

① Sew.

body (wrong side)

fusible fabric

① Sew.

② Notch the margins   ③ Open the seam

Lining of body (right side)

Turn on the right side

② Sew   0.3 cm

body (right side)

Lining of the body (wrong side)

② Sew   0.3 cm

2 SEW THE SIDES OF THE BODY

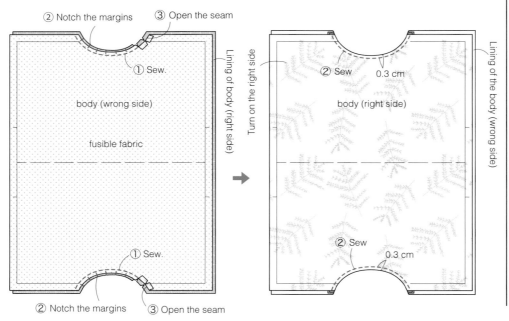

Set aside the lining

lining of the body (wrong side)

② Sew

② Sew

body (wrong side)

① Turn right side out then fold in half

③ Cut the corners of the margins

3 SEW THE SIDES OF THE LINING BODY

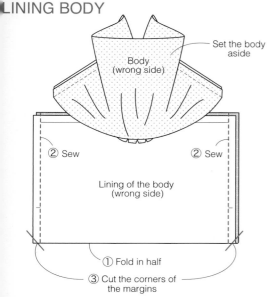

Set the body aside

Body (wrong side)

② Sew   ② Sew

Lining of the body (wrong side)

① Fold in half

③ Cut the corners of the margins

4 SEW THE BELLOWS

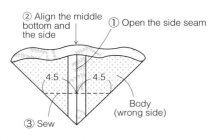

② Align the middle bottom and the side   ① Open the side seam

4.5   4.5

③ Sew

Body (wrong side)

※ Sew the other pocket in the same way.

5 ASSEMBLE THE BODY AND THE LINING, RIGHT SIDES TOGETHER, THEN SEW THE MARGINS

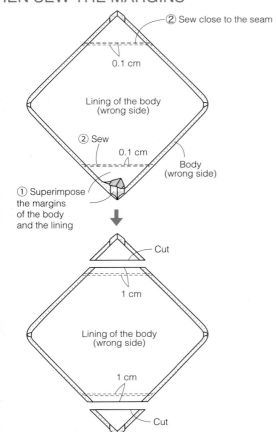

② Sew close to the seam

0.1 cm

Lining of the body (wrong side)

② Sew

0.1 cm

Body (wrong side)

① Superimpose the margins of the body and the lining

Cut

1 cm

Lining of the body (wrong side)

1 cm

Cut

6 TURN THE BODY ON THE RIGHT SIDE, THEN POKE THE OPENING

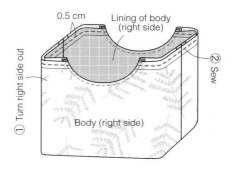

0.5 cm   Lining of body (right side)

① Turn right side out

② Sew

Body (right side)

7 MAKE THE HANDLE

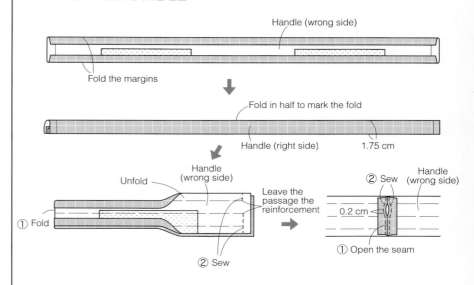

Handle (wrong side)

Fold the margins

Fold in half to mark the fold

Handle (right side)   1.75 cm

Unfold   Handle (wrong side)

Leave the passage the reinforcement

② Sew   Handle (wrong side)

0.2 cm

① Fold

② Sew

① Open the seam

8 SEW THE HANDLE ONTO THE BODY

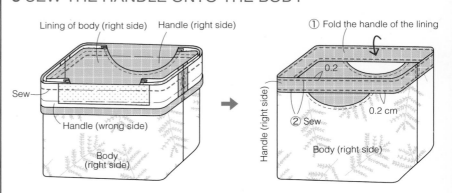

Lining of body (right side)   Handle (right side)   ① Fold the handle of the lining

Sew

Handle (wrong side)

0.2

0.2 cm

② Sew

Handle (right side)

Body (right side)

Body (right side)

9 INSERT THE METAL REINFORCEMENTS

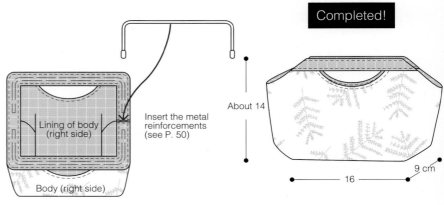

Completed!

Lining of body (right side)

Insert the metal reinforcements (see P. 50)

Body (right side)

About 14

16   9 cm

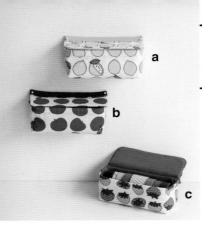

a

b

c

WALL STORAGE BOXES
NO 18 PAGE 45

(Body, body lining, flap, flap lining)

SUPPLIES

(for 1 model, from left to right for models a / b / c)
20 x 45 cm of cotton printed with lemons / apples / strawberries (fabric A)
20 x 45 cm of Oxford yellow / blue / red (fabric B)
20 x 50 cm of fusible interlining
1 pair of metal reinforcements 5 x 15 cm

PREPARATION

Heat seal the body and the flap.

※ There is no pattern for the border for this model.
Mark it directly on the fabric.
※ The numbers in the square correspond to the seam margins.
Add 1 cm margin, unless otherwise indicated.
※ Heat-seal the blue parts. ⬚

Cutting Plans

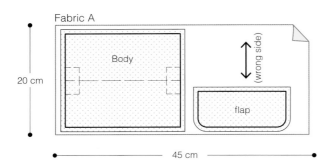

Fabric A

20 cm

Body

(wrong side)

flap

45 cm

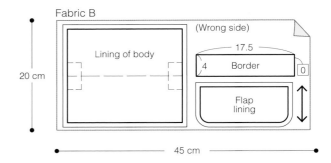

Fabric B

(Wrong side)

20 cm

Lining of body

17.5

4 Border 0

Flap lining

45 cm

CONSTRUCTION

1 SEW THE SIDES OF THE BODY

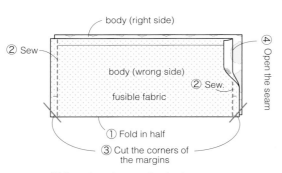

body (right side)

② Sew

body (wrong side)

fusible fabric

② Sew.

④ Open the seam

① Fold in half

③ Cut the corners of the margins

※ Sew the other pocket in the same way.

2 SEW THE BELLOWS

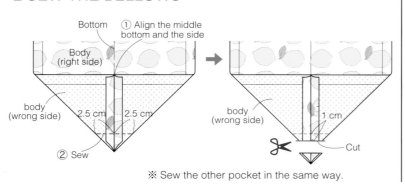

Bottom

① Align the middle bottom and the side

Body (right side)

body (wrong side)

2.5 cm 2.5 cm

② Sew

body (wrong side)

1 cm

Cut

※ Sew the other pocket in the same way.

3 MAKE THE FLAP

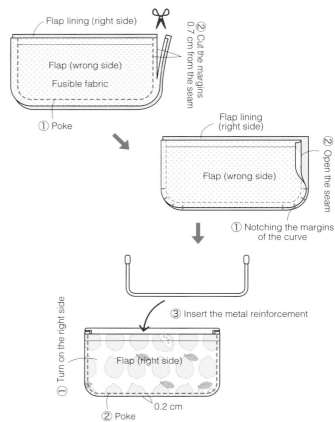

Flap lining (right side)

✂

② Cut the margins 0.7 cm from the seam

Flap (wrong side)

Fusible fabric

① Poke

Flap lining (right side)

② Open the seam

Flap (wrong side)

① Notching the margins of the curve

① Turn on the right side

③ Insert the metal reinforcement

Flap (right side)

0.2 cm

② Poke

4 SUPERIMPOSE THE BODY AND THE LINING, RIGHT SIDES TOGETHER, THEN SEW THE OPENING

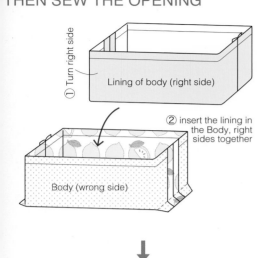

① Turn right side

Lining of body (right side)

② insert the lining in the Body, right sides together

Body (wrong side)

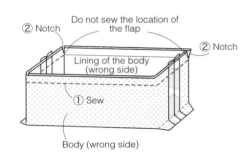

② Notch

Do not sew the location of the flap

② Notch

Lining of the body (wrong side)

① Sew

Body (wrong side)

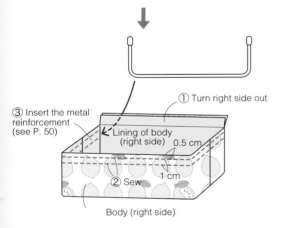

① Turn right side out

③ Insert the metal reinforcement (see P. 50)

Lining of body (right side)

0.5 cm

② Sew

1 cm

Body (right side)

5 SEW THE FLAP ON THE BODY

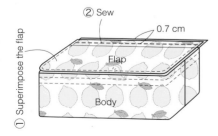

② Sew

0.7 cm

Flap

① Superimpose the flap

Body

6 SEW THE BORDER

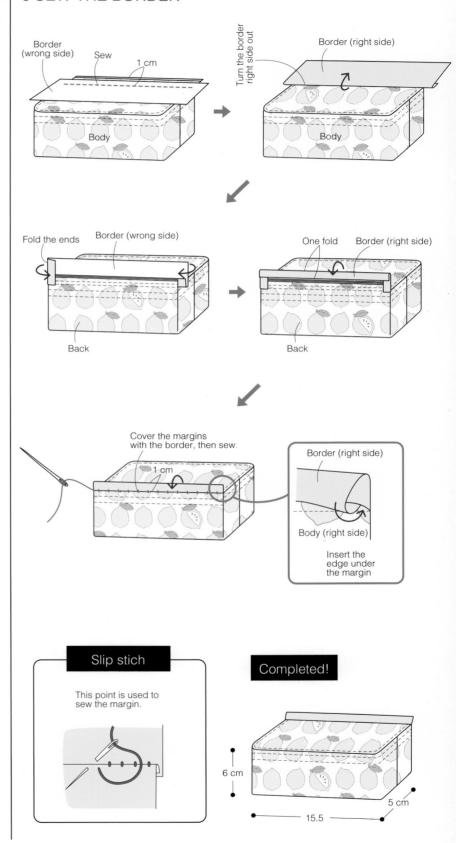

Border (wrong side)

Sew

1 cm

Body

Turn the border right side out

Border (right side)

Body

Fold the ends

Border (wrong side)

Back

One fold

Border (right side)

Back

Cover the margins with the border, then sew.

1 cm

Border (right side)

Body (right side)

Insert the edge under the margin

Slip stich

This point is used to sew the margin.

Completed!

6 cm

5 cm

15.5

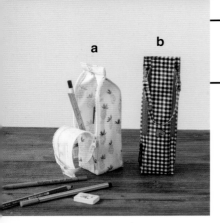

PENCIL CASES
NO 19 PAGE 46

SUPPLIES (a)

40 x 40 cm of pineapple printed oilcloth (fabric A)
2 zippers 12 cm long
20 cm of ecru twill ribbon 2 cm wide
1 pair of magnets ø 0.5 cm
1 label of 1.5 x 4.5 cm

SUPPLIES (b)

40 x 40 cm of hearts printed oilcloth (fabric A)
2 zippers 12 cm long
20 cm of ecru twill ribbon 2 cm wide
1 pair of magnets ø 0.5 cm
1 label of 1.5 x 4 cm

Cutting Plans

※ There is no pattern for this model.
Trace them directly onto the fabric.
※ The numbers in the square correspond
to the seam margins.
Add 1 cm margin, unless otherwise indicated.

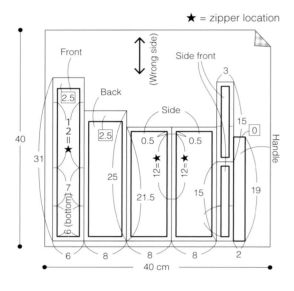

2 ASSEMBLE THE FRONT AND THE PARTS FROM STEP 1

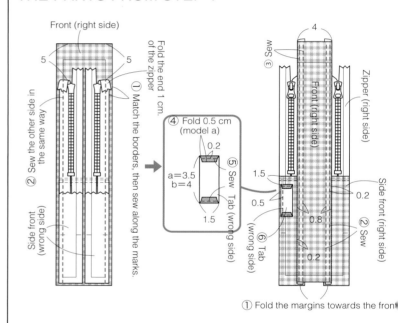

CONSTRUCTION

1 SEW THE ZIPPER AND THE FRONT SIDE

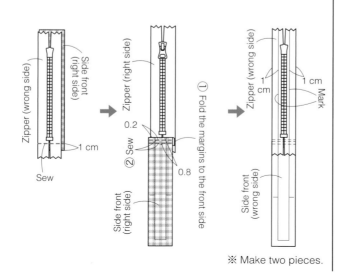

3 SEW THE BOTTOM OF THE FRONT AND BACK

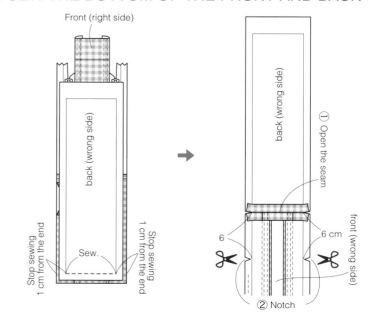

4 SEW THE BOTTOM OF THE FRONT AND SIDES

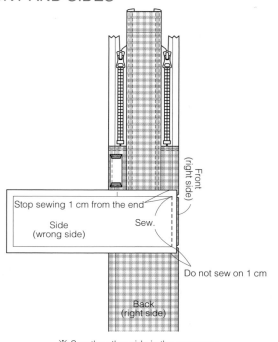

Stop sewing 1 cm from the end

Side (wrong side)

Sew.

Front (right side)

Do not sew on 1 cm

Back (right side)

※ Sew the other side in the same way.

5 ASSEMBLE THE BACK AND THE SIDES

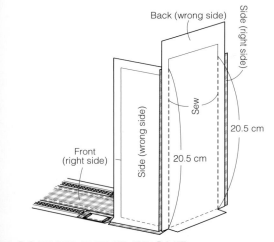

Back (wrong side)

Side (right side)

Side (wrong side)

Sew

20.5 cm

20.5 cm

Front (right side)

6 ASSEMBLE THE FRONT AND THE SIDES

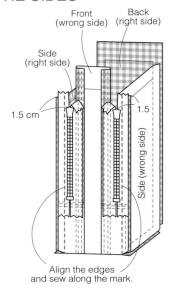

Front (wrong side)

Back (right side)

Side (right side)

Side (wrong side)

1.5 cm

1.5

Align the edges and sew along the mark.

7 SEW THE CORNERS OF THE BACK AND SIDES FOLD THE SIDES, THEN SEW THE TOP

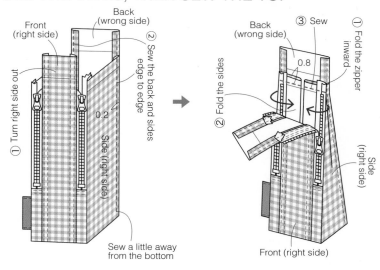

Front (right side)

Back (wrong side)

② Sew the back and sides edge to edge

① Turn right side out

0.2

Side (right side)

Back (wrong side)

③ Sew

0.8

① Fold the zipper inward

② Fold the sides

Side (right side)

Front (right side)

Sew a little away from the bottom

8 MAKE THE STRIP FOR THE MAGNETS

※ See P. 51

9 FIX THE MAGNETS

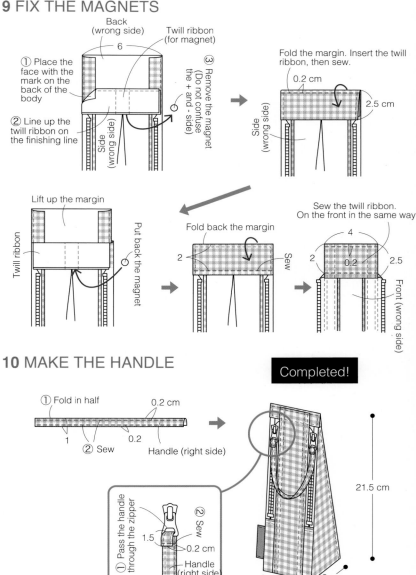

Back (wrong side)

6

Twill ribbon (for magnet)

① Place the face with the mark on the back of the body

② Line up the twill ribbon on the finishing line

Side (wrong side)

③ Remove the magnet (Do not confuse the + and - side)

Fold the margin. Insert the twill ribbon, then sew.

0.2 cm

2.5 cm

Side (wrong side)

Lift up the margin

Twill ribbon

Put back the magnet

Fold back the margin

2

Sew

Sew the twill ribbon. On the front in the same way

4

2

0.2

2.5

Front (wrong side)

10 MAKE THE HANDLE

① Fold in half

0.2 cm

1

② Sew

0.2

Handle (right side)

Completed!

① Pass the handle through the zipper

② Sew

1.5

0.2 cm

Handle (right side)

21.5 cm

6

6 cm

Tuva Publishing
www.tuvapublishing.com

Address Merkez Mah. Cavusbasi Cad. No71
Cekmekoy - Istanbul 34782 / Turkey
Tel +9 0216 642 62 62

Sew Your Own Bags and Accessories

First Print 2021 / March

All Global Copyrights Belong To
Tuva Tekstil ve Yayıncılık Ltd.

Content Sewing

Editor in Chief Ayhan DEMİRPEHLİVAN
Project Editor Kader DEMİRPEHLİVAN
Author Shufuno MISHIN
Technical Editors Leyla ARAS, Büşra ESER
Graphic Designers Ömer ALP, Abdullah BAYRAKÇI, Tarık TOKGÖZ

ISBN 978-605-78-34-21-8

Lady Boutique Series No.4807
Shufuno Mishin Omoshiroi Shikakeno Nunokomono
Copyright © Boutique-sha, Inc. 2019
Original Japanese edition published in Japan by Boutique-sha, Inc.
English translation rights arranged with Boutique-sha, Inc.

 TuvaYayincilik TuvaPublishing
 TuvaYayincilik TuvaPublishing